LOST & FOUND:

A MOTHER AND SON FIND VICTORY OVER TEEN DRUG ADDICTION

IMPORTANT INFORMATION & RESOURCES EVERY PARENT SHOULD HAVE

CHRISTY CRANDELL
WITH CYNTHIA CUTTS

Pascoe Publishing, Inc.
Rocklin, California

Disclaimer:
The information included in this book is a true account of teenage drug addiction. The advice offered is in no way intended to diagnose, treat or counsel drug-addicted individuals or their families. The ideas and suggestions contained in this book are not intended as a substitute for consulting with a physician, counselor or drug treatment professional. Always consult a physician in matters relating to your health. Likewise, if you feel desperate and are unable to cope with stressful events, you should seek help from a qualified health care provider.

Cover and Interior Design by Kayla Blanco

Published in the United States of America by

 Pascoe Publishing, Inc.
Rocklin, California
www.pascoepublishing.com

06   07   08   09   8   7   6   5   4   3   2   1

Printed in China

This book is dedicated to my son, Ryan, who has triumphed over drug addiction and matured into a wonderful young man. Throughout the pain of losing Ryan to drugs, I always loved him and I never gave up on him. His battle with addiction, his crimes and imprisonment were the most difficult things I've endured in my life. Yet, walking the dark valleys of Ryan's addiction has made me a more accepting, understanding and compassionate person. I'll always love you, Ryan, and I look forward to the day I can bring you home.

Christy Crandell

ACKNOWLEDGMENTS

The journey of Ryan's addiction and incarceration would never have been bearable without the love and support of my husband, Rick, and son, Justin. Over the past three years, my family and close friends have helped me heal from the tragedy of Ryan's drug addiction, arrest and prison sentence. I am convinced that I have survived this heartbreak as a result of the constant outpouring of their love and prayers. The idea of writing a book about my experiences required that I return to a place of pain and anguish that I didn't want to revisit. Many thanks to my developmental editor, Cynthia Cutts, who patiently and compassionately pulled the dark details of this story from me. She turned my thoughts into a book I hope will help other families avoid a similar tragedy.

I am also honored to work with Debbie Parisi, my marketing and public relations consultant, and Karen Pascoe and Debi Bock at Pascoe Publishing, Inc., who appreciated the value of my story and shared my goal of getting this information into the hands of parents. Their encouragement, kind words and enthusiasm have made the task of writing this book a pleasure.

—Christy Crandell

TABLE OF CONTENTS:

FOREWORD

By Ryan Crandell

"Put your hands up! Get out of the car slowly! Get down on your hands and knees. Anyone else in the car?" A deputy sheriff pointed a gun at me as he gave orders. A large, barking police dog lunged toward me, tugging fiercely at the end of a leash. I got out of the car and $200 in cash floated to the ground. It was money I had taken when I'd robbed a bookstore just hours earlier. I'd already spent the cash from the other four armed robberies I'd committed within the past 48 hours. I'd been in a drug-induced cloud of Coricidin and marijuana for the past three months and my mind was foggy. Handcuffed, I was loaded into the sheriff's cruiser to begin what would evolve into a 13-year prison sentence in a California State Penitentiary. I was three weeks past my 18th birthday.

I wasn't even supposed to be where the robberies started. When I'd left my house in Rocklin, California, my plan was to drive to Carson City, Nevada and stay with the family of a girl I'd met while in rehab. I even had a job lined up at a lumber company. That was honestly my intention—to go live in Nevada, away from all the drugs and people in my home town who used drugs. I now think about how different my life might be had I headed there directly. Unfortunately, I made a big detour with life-changing consequences.

How did this happen to me? I had a great childhood. My father coached my sports teams and my mother was always up to cook breakfast, take me to school and take care of me. There was no dysfunctional family on whom to blame my problems. I had loving parents, a great little brother, a nice home, a cool car and plenty of advantages. If I had to sum up my family life in one word it would be "awesome."

I suppose I started like a lot of kids do—in their parents' liquor cabinet. From there, I progressed to marijuana and eventually became addicted to drugs. I used anything I could get my hands on, often mixing over-the-counter cold medications with alcohol or illegal drugs. As my drug habits progressed, I began stealing from my parents' wallets. I argued about everything and skipped school. I hid my drug habits well and became a proficient liar. But, eventually the truth of my addiction was revealed and I was placed in a drug treatment facility.

Despite repeated drug rehabilitation efforts, I could only stay clean and sober for 67 days before the overwhelming pull of drugs lured me back into its deceptive grip. And, during the three months before being arrested for armed robbery, I was high 24/7. Don't ask me what I was thinking during those five armed robberies. I wasn't thinking. I was in a drug-induced haze. About the only thing I remember was driving on the freeway, feeling like I was in a video game, racing down the road, trying to stay between the dotted lines.

I'll be in prison until I'm 31 years old. I'll do the time I owe the state and then start my life again. I take full responsibility for my crimes and I deserve to be behind bars. No one is to blame for my situation except me. If I hadn't been arrested, I'd be dead because of my drug addiction and things I did to support that addiction. One day I hope to get out of prison and become a drug and alcohol counselor. I think that I can help an addict better than someone else who hasn't walked in that dark valley of shadows the way I have.

I've put my family through hell. And I don't deserve their love. Amazingly, they have forgiven me and for that I am extremely grateful. My promise to my family is to stay clean for the rest of my life, one day at a time. I've rededicated my life to God, and with His help, I know that it is definitely possible.

My mom, a very wise woman whom I love and respect, once told me that God's plan is perfect; that everything happens for a reason, and that God will never give me more than I can bear. She's now written this book about what she's learned through my drug addiction and has dedicated her life to preventing other teenagers from going through the same tragedy that I took my family through. I'm so proud of her.

This is a true story of how I screwed up. But it's also filled with good advice from my mom, who learned the hard way, as she tried to help me beat drugs. Every parent needs the information on these pages. If you're a parent, you need to be informed about how easy it is for kids to get hooked on drugs and alcohol and what you can do to help your kids when it happens.

Ryan

INTRODUCTION

PARENTS, PAY ATTENTION TO THIS BOOK!

The biggest parenting fallacy in the world lies in thinking that we can somehow protect our children by living in nice houses, in nice neighborhoods, in quiet little towns—and by thinking the walls of our houses will protect our children from making big decisions! They won't! Our children will make ALL of the big decisions in their lives. I simply cannot say it any more forcefully! If you have not yet realized that the decision about using drugs poses a threat to every single child, wake up!

Over the past 10 years, as I have taught parents HOW to teach their children to make good decisions via my Parenting with Dignity curriculum, I have told these parents the one thing I know to be the absolute truth: "Your children will make all the big decisions in their lives, not some—all. When they make the decision about whether they will use cocaine, marijuana, methamphetamines, alcohol, or any other drug, you will not be present and therefore you will be unable to protect them. The person offering the drug will make sure you are not there!"

What our children will use to make those decisions will hopefully be what we have taught them. However, our failure to teach them how to make those decisions does not mean they will not make them! It just means that they will use ideas someone else has taught them about using illegal substances. And, believe me, what some of the other people will teach them is not what you want them using to make that life or death decision.

I wish that I could get every parent to read this book. My wish is that every parent would read this book at the time their first child is born! Then, maybe they could see, first hand, how the tragedy of drug addiction can strike any child who is not completely and totally well-prepared with good decision-making skills.

Living in a home with loving parents who have strong morals and ethics is not the same as teaching a child how to use those ideas to make good decisions. As I tell parents over and over, "Talking is not teaching. Telling is not teaching. What you are doing does not become teaching until you see change as a result."

This book should serve as a wake-up call to every parent who is raising a child. Most of life's good decisions are made in our heads BEFORE we are in the situation. Our children are no different and they cannot be allowed to wait until they are in a situation like the Crandell family, before they are taught how to make good decisions for themselves based upon sound morals, values, ethics and principles.

Hopefully, this book will help parents realize that, without proper awareness and a sound plan for teaching their children, drug addiction and the pain and misery associated with it, is a very real possibility for their children and their family.

Please read this book and learn from the heartache and pain the Crandell family has experienced. Then, please share this book with every parent you know so that they can be aware of what may be waiting for them if they do not act now to teach their children how to make big decisions.

MAC BLEDSOE, PRESIDENT and FOUNDER
Drew Bledsoe Foundation

Mac Bledsoe is the author of the parenting curriculum and book titled, *Parenting with Dignity*. Mac's son, famed professional football player, Drew Bledsoe, established the foundation to address issues confronting today's youth. Mac's parenting expertise is based on his 30 years of teaching high school and coaching sports and 19 years conducting parenting workshops around the country. His curriculum received national exposure when it was featured on ABC's 20/20.

To find out more about *Parenting with Dignity*, please visit
www.parentingwithdignity.com

ONE

THE DARKEST DAY OF MY LIFE

It was the day I wished my son had died. It was the darkest day of my life. I remember it with a black-draped sadness that still hurts my heart. I'd been on an overnight girls' getaway with my mother and sister. Just before we left, my 18-year-old son, Ryan was in crisis again and I wasn't really enjoying the trip. I asked to come home early and my mom and sister agreed. When I got to my house, no one was home. And when I reviewed the messages on the answering machine, I discovered a call from the Nevada County Sheriff's Office that had been left at 4 a.m. that morning. I knew nothing good could have come from that message.

My husband, Rick, and son, Justin, came home from church that morning to gently break the news to me that Ryan had been arrested for five counts of armed robbery. My son had been part of a dangerous crime spree through the Sierra Nevada foothills that included multiple felonies with weapons and drugs. Just three weeks past his 18th birthday, Ryan was legally an "adult" and, with three minors involved, the law considered him the adult responsible for the welfare of the others. Ryan was in serious trouble—trouble that would ultimately earn him 13 years in the California State Penitentiary.

When I first heard what Ryan had done, I honestly wished he had died. As the panic and despair roared through my heart, I remember saying as much to my husband. I was thinking about the bleak future ahead for Ryan; a cold cell, a taunting drug addiction, despairing loneliness, intense pain. I thought of him enduring all of that without us and I kept saying, "It would be better for Ryan if he had died. If that had happened he wouldn't be in pain, he wouldn't be suffering from drug addiction, he wouldn't be so desperately unhappy."

I believed that, if Ryan had died, he would have been a saved soul. He wasn't living the life of a Christian, but I remember when he was 9 years old, right after Bible camp, sitting on the front lawn, he asked Jesus into his heart. I knew Ryan belonged to God and I knew that he would remain in God's care even if he had pulled away from his faith. And, at the moment of this crisis, I truly wished Ryan had been taken home to heaven rather than face the traumatic consequences of his crimes here on earth.

As Rick took care of the details involved in hiring a defense attorney, I went into an emotional state of shock that put me into a gray mental fog. I could not wrap my mind around what law enforcement officials were saying my son had done. Ryan was charged with armed robbery. He had held up convenience stores, gas stations and a bookstore with a gun and a knife. No one was injured, assaulted or physically harmed, but witnesses said Ryan shot a gun into the air as he left the scene of one crime. This was not the Ryan I knew and loved. This was not the Ryan I'd raised for 18 years. This was not something that could even possibly happen to our family.

In my emotional distress, simple things like eating and basic hygiene became unimportant to me. I had fearful visions revolving throughout my mind of Ryan, terrified and confused, in a jail cell, cold and hungry, and I could not get to him. I wasn't allowed to see Ryan, contact him or touch him. Ryan was an adult in jail. Moms don't have clout when they have a child in jail. From a mother's standpoint, I'd always taken care of Ryan's basic needs and now I was unable to do anything for him. Despite all of our earlier conflicts and crises with drugs through the recent years, Ryan had been living at home and I was still his primary care-giver. The thought that I couldn't help Ryan when he needed help the most was more than I could bear.

The worst of it was looking back during those dark hours, as I recognized how desperate Ryan had been during the prior months and years. It was brutal to realize that I had simply missed all the classic symptoms and signals of drug addiction and all of Ryan's desperate cries for help. I realized that, had I done things differently with Ryan, this tragedy might have been prevented. I had been a good mother. Rick and I were active, interested and caring parents. We lived in an upscale, safe neighborhood. Our home was a strong, stable environment where our sons could thrive. But we made major mistakes when Ryan chose a path of drugs and alcohol.

I wish I'd known...Local statistics in our low-crime county indicate that 85% of teenagers regularly use alcohol or drugs. While this statistic is alarming, what is even more alarming is that, when polled, teenagers not only agree with that statistic, they believe it might be too low.

I wish I'd known...I had no point of reference for teenage drug addiction or alcohol abuse. Yet, there are currently more than 10 million alcohol drinkers in the United States who are between the ages of 12 and 20 years old.

I wish I'd known...that people with a history of drug abuse in their families are more susceptible to also developing problems with addiction. Children of alcoholics or addicts are three times more likely to develop addiction problems. If both parents are addicts or alcoholics, the risk increases five times!

Even though Rick and I have never struggled with addiction ourselves, it is certainly evident in our family history.

TWO

A Loving Home and a Secure Life

Armed robbery was never on my "worry list." Drug addiction wasn't on the list, either. As a devoted mother, I had lots of concerns about raising my boys in our fast paced, high-demand world. I worried about getting them into the right college and getting a good job. I worried about driving too fast, car accidents and getting the flu. I worried about too many girlfriends, or maybe not making the best choices with the ones they had. Armed robbery and drug addiction weren't even on my radar screen of worry.

All my life I wanted to be a mom. When I was a young girl and thought of my future, being a mother was what I pictured. Maybe that's why I married early—to get to my dream faster. After 18 hours of labor, when Ryan was first handed to me, I never expected to feel so much love so fast. From that day on, I was on a mission to be the best mother I could possibly be. I had no idea the job was going to be so hard, nor did I ever imagine it would be filled with so much pain and heartache. I had been given the perfect example of how to raise a family by my own mother and father. I grew up in a traditional, loving home with two parents who loved me and each other. When I planned my future, I always intended to be a stay-at-home mom. My devoted husband, Rick, was equally committed to having me stay at home with our children. Our two adorable, dark haired, fair-skinned sons, Ryan and Justin, were born two and a half years apart and I loved taking care of them. I often marveled at how perfectly satisfying it was to live my dream with Rick.

When we were first married, Rick was able to secure a great job, but he was also willing to work additional jobs to keep our family grounded in the values we cherished. Both Rick and I were active in our community, taking on countless leadership roles. I volunteered in classroom activities, chaperoned all the boys' field trips, and was a room mother, team mother and "emergency mother" for many children. I served as president of the PTC, nationally known as PTA, was active in our church, and on the Little League Board of Directors, and our house was always filled with kids after school. Although Rick worked full-time and sometimes at additional jobs, he still found time to coach the boys' youth sports teams. We were both active in civic events. Our marriage was always strong, with both of us dedicated to family harmony, unity and cohesiveness.

We lived in Rocklin, California, a small, friendly, upscale, middle-class suburban community about 25 miles northeast of California's capital city, Sacramento. When Ryan was 3, Rick and I decided that Rocklin was the perfect community in which to raise our boys. It was a sort of "Mayberry" town, nestled in the foothills of the Sierra Mountains, where neighbors knew neighbors, and "law enforcement" usually meant speeding tickets or citations for barking dogs.

Families in Rocklin were more often than not, two-parent homes with well-paying careers. Within our neighborhood were engineers, health care professionals, police officers, firemen, college professors, CEOs, professional athletes, teachers, school administrators, television and radio personalities, airline pilots, military officers and many other highly respected professionals.

Parents in our neighborhood had high expectations for their children and provided support for those expectations. Children were encouraged to develop their talents and interests. Children went to summer camps, played on AAU sports teams and worked with sports specialists to improve their abilities. College goals were set for kids in our neighborhood at an early age. If you grew up in Rocklin, there was plenty of support for you to reach a lofty goal as an adult. I thought Rocklin was the best of both worlds. It was close enough to San Francisco to provide those big city opportunities such as museums, the theatre or professional baseball outings, yet far enough away to be safe from that big city influence. It was close enough to be considered a Sacramento suburb and many people in Rocklin commuted daily to downtown Sacramento, yet Rocklin offered a culture of an insulated and almost rural community.

Rocklin was a tidy, little town of new homes with flowering plum trees lining the streets, lush landscaped curbs, sidewalks and crosswalks. It was a town with graffiti-free schools where kids walked or rode their bikes to school, crossed the street with a crossing guard, said the Pledge of Allegiance every day, enrolled in the DARE program, studied art, music, physical education and the environment. Our neighborhood school was a place where third graders put on the musical "Going Buggy," and fourth graders spent the night at Sutter's Fort to experience the California gold rush.

In Rocklin, the biggest community celebration was just before the Fourth of July with a parade, a barbecue and fireworks in the park. Crime in Rocklin was minimal and it was easy to isolate our family from whatever crime was reported in Rocklin. Our police department proudly reported a zero tolerance for gangs while teaching Neighborhood Watch programs. Rocklin had a comfortable public library with reading programs to inspire young readers, as well as regular art shows where local artists could showcase their work. City council members were visible, active volunteers, hosting charity events, while extolling the virtues of their political platforms. Rocklin had a community newspaper which reported local news, social events, reviewed local performing arts and celebrated victories of youth sports. My sons looked forward to finding their photos in our newspaper after winning a championship game.

Our home was full of love, laughter and security. Our neighborhood was safe, filled with children the same age as my boys, who were in and out of each other's homes all day long. We had block parties, pool parties, barbeques and our sons enjoyed a very nurturing neighborhood culture. Our lifestyle was a step back in time, to a simpler day when neighbors shared their daily lives with each other. I was so grateful that Rick and I were able to provide this lifestyle for our boys, so that they could grow up to be connected to their community. We wanted the boys to grow up to be responsible citizens and thought Rocklin provided a culture to foster that hope.

Rick and I worked hard to be an integral part of each of our sons' lives. When the boys were in elementary school, we practiced spelling words, rehearsed presentations, helped with props and costumes for projects and supported the boys throughout their education. Both of my boys took pride in their homework and were extremely successful students. Each of them regularly brought home glowing report cards. It's funny now to think back how citizenship reports for Ryan always indicated that he was a good citizen, but they were usually also tinged with a little bit of concern that he could improve on self-control.

Rick and I told or read bedtime stories, said prayers as we tucked the boys in at night, and tickled their arms softly to relax them. We encouraged the boys' dreams and provided opportunities to develop their talents. We didn't spoil them, but we did provide the boys with many advantages such as baseball and football camps, swimming lessons, gym memberships and gymnastics lessons. We took them to church and tried to model strong moral values.

Rick and I developed family traditions that often mirrored a Norman Rockwell painting. Easter traditions included the Easter Bunny hiding the boys' baskets and the first part of the morning was spent looking for them. After church, we would gather with my family and the neighborhood and have a big Easter egg hunt, spread over the lawns of our nearest neighbors.

Until the boys were about 11 and 14, every year we'd have a family reunion in Oregon during the Fourth of July weekend. There we would hold our own family Fourth of July Olympics. Ryan's grandparents lived on 26 acres, where we played Frisbee golf, croquet, volleyball, horseshoes, bocce ball, lawn darts, bubble gum blowing contests and we even received spirit points for Fourth of July apparel. Everyone in the family competed for a coveted plastic Olympic trophy. It was an annual event that Rick, Ryan, Justin and I looked forward to and celebrated.

Thanksgiving was also a big family event with a traditional dinner. We'd sit around a table loaded with turkey, mashed potatoes, sweet potatoes, green bean casserole and cranberry sauce and we'd say grace before we ate. Then, each of the 22 of us, still holding hands, would share individually and say what we were thankful for. In addition to special family vacations and other holidays, Christmas was the highlight of our year. Our Christmases included making a trip to the Sierra or Cascade Mountains to cut our own tree. We'd decorate the tree with favorite ornaments that had been lovingly preserved each year since the boys were babies. The boys would compete for the "front of the tree" position with their personalized photo ornaments, jockeying to see whose ornament was the most visible from across the room.

After Christmas Eve services, we'd come home to open one gift and then, on Christmas mornings, we'd open the remaining gifts from Santa and have breakfast. After breakfast, we'd go back to the tree to open more gifts. Christmas gifts for the boys might include bikes, a video or computer game system, an electronic basketball hoop or personal stereos. The boys always presented hand-made gifts for our extended family and would barely be able to wait as these special gifts were opened one by one. We could easily extend our Christmas morning gift exchange until late morning and the rest of the day was spent with family enjoying new games or toys. The day would end with a big Christmas dinner including a honey-baked ham and all the trimmings.

Our family vacations were usually spent with close family friends and Lake Tahoe was one of our favorite destinations. We played cards and board games and spent time at the beach. We rented kayaks and jet skis. We also regularly visited my parents in Oregon, where we would go white water rafting. Once, on a bet from my cousin, Ryan jumped off a 30-foot cliff into the Rogue River and lived to collect his money. When the boys were 10 and 13, we took them to Orlando, Florida to Disney World, where we stayed at a resort with a lake. Unbelievably, 13 years old was old enough to rent a motor boat, so Ryan and Justin immediately wanted to rent one. Ryan and Justin went out and, because of Ryan's need for the thrill of speed, he pulled the boat throttle as fast as the boat could go. He found out quickly, however, that a boat doesn't respond to turns as rapidly as a bike and he clipped another family in a paddle boat. No one was hurt, but it was still scary and embarrassing as Rick and I watched in horror from the safety of another boat.

We had other family traditions, including the annual first day of school photos. Every year, from Ryan's first day of kindergarten on, I'd line up the neighborhood kids and take a photo to remember the day. All the neighborhood moms and dads would meet in front of our house on that first day of school to take a medley of photos. Each child would have a new backpack, new lunch box, new haircut, new school outfit and a grin in anticipation of the new school year—as the cameras clicked away.

Every night, our family sat around the table for dinner. We'd engage in what we called, "Good Day, Bad Day," which was a way to debrief and connect our days. It opened up channels of information for the kids that demonstrated the reality of adulthood and the good and bad things that can happen at any age. This little exercise helped prevent the single word answer, "nothing" when we asked our boys about their days. It also allowed them to share both the good and the bad of their days. Rick usually said the "good" part of his day was sitting around the table with us during that dinner.

Our family developed all sorts of wacky games with the boys. They loved to play Stuffed Animal Dodge Ball with Rick and I, where they'd circle the rooms as we'd try to tag them with soft, stuffed animals. They'd race around and around the house until they tired out and were ready for bed. Ryan and Justin made forts with sheets where they'd have snacks, then slide down the stairs on bean bags or pillow cases. As the boys got older and developed friendships outside of our family, Sunday nights were designated "family game night." Each week one of us was allowed to choose what our family activity would be—a board game, card game or a movie. Together, over the summer, our family listened as I read *Where the Red Fern Grows* and *James and the Giant Peach*.

Rick grew up as a fan of the major league baseball Giants team. Because of this, our boys were outfitted in Giants shirts and hats early in their lives. Since Rick had played both high school and college baseball, he was eager to encourage our boys' athletic talents. Rick nurtured their competitive natures and was able to coach them in Little League and Junior League Football. After each competition, our whole family enjoyed reviewing game films and recapping the games, play by play.

I always knew we had a great lifestyle and I don't think I ever took it for granted. The main ingredient our boys had in their lives was love. They knew that Rick and I were totally devoted to them and that we loved them. But, the truth is, even with all of the love and security we gave to our sons, it was not enough to prevent Ryan's choices.

> *I wish I'd known...Drug addiction respects no economic, educational or moral value boundaries. Drug addiction happens to people from all walks of life. There is no safe place to live to protect your children from drug addiction.*
>
> *I wish I'd known...Drug addiction is a progressive disease and can be fatal if left untreated. A study prepared in 2002 by the Office of National Drug Control Policy estimated the total economic costs of alcohol and drug abuse in the United States to be $180.9 billion for that year alone.*

Ryan was a strong, dynamic personality from day one. I always said that he came out of the womb "hard." Emotionally, Ryan was either really up or really down. There wasn't a lot of in-between with Ryan. He gave me my highest highs and my lowest lows. Ryan was always testing the limits and he always had to learn "the hard way."

While being Ryan's mother was challenging for me, he had many endearing qualities. His intense sense of justice was matched only by his extreme sensitivity. At a very young age, he had a keen awareness of the feelings and attitudes of others that far exceeded his years. Ryan was always on the lookout for the underdog, ready to defend him without regard for what it might do to his own status. His best friend lived across the street from us and was afflicted with selective mutism. This is an anxiety disorder characterized by the child's inability to speak in social situations. Ryan was the only person this child would speak to. When the boys went to school Ryan spoke for him, looked out for him on the playground and was his self-appointed guardian. No one asked Ryan to do this, but Ryan was a loyal comrade and decided to look after his best friend on his own.

Ryan was always watching out for the feelings of others. I recall picture day in kindergarten when I was helping the children as they prepared for their classroom photograph. Next to Ryan were Ashley and Kaitlin, two little girls from his classroom. As I reached out and straightened the collar on Ashley's shirt, I commented, "Oh Ashley, you look so pretty today." And before I had the words out, Ryan piped up with, "Yes, Mom, and Kaitlin looks very pretty today, too." It floored me that a six-year-old was that sensitive to the feelings of a little girl who might have felt slighted or hurt by being left out of the compliment.

Ryan told me the good and the bad—sometimes things I didn't even want to know. If he did something wrong as a child, he had an extremely guilty conscience. He would confess to his misdeeds willingly. At age 11, he and his friends were throwing rocks on a construction site and broke the window on a tractor. He waited a few days, but then came to me to confess, feeling too guilty to keep it all inside. Looking back at all the wrongs to which Ryan later confessed, I know how difficult it had to be for him to carry them on his conscience.

Ryan had an unusual energy about him that was electric. You could feel Ryan's presence when he entered a room. He was always extreme; extremely happy about something or extremely unhappy about something. Ryan's conversations always ended with exclamation points. He wore his emotions on his sleeve. Ryan and I had a very close relationship. I never had to guess what his stand was on issues or what he was feeling. Ryan shared things openly and unabashedly. When I looked back, I was baffled by the fact that I didn't have to ask questions or pry into Ryan's life. He "spilled his guts" every day. So, when I look back now and realize how many heart-to-heart conversations we'd had, I am amazed at how good Ryan became at lying or telling his "version" of the truth.

I could ask Ryan, "Would you like a cookie?" when he was three or four years old. And Ryan would say, "No, I want two cookies."
And the battle would begin, with me saying, "No, you get one or none."
And Ryan, negotiating a way to have two.
He could be exhausting.

I wish I'd known...a classic ingredient for drug abuse is lying. Drugs help you lie. When a teen is using drugs and hiding it from parents, he or she become like a "secret agent" to cover up any signs of use. Teens who use drugs say that their main concern isn't the debilitating effect of drugs on their bodies, or even being arrested. Their biggest concern is getting caught with drugs by their parents.

I wish I'd known...about the importance of "Caller ID." To ensure that your child is really where he says he is, don't rely on cell phone calls to verify his whereabouts. Invest in "Caller ID" for your land phone line and insist that your son or daughter call you from the home where he or she is supposed to be. "Caller ID" will confirm that your child is not calling from a different location.

I wish I'd known...about My Space, an extremely popular teen website that allows you, as a parent, to navigate through web pages created by your child and his or her friends. This glimpse into their lives and culture will help you assess your child's behavior and that of his friends. Register to open your account at www.myspace.com.

I wish I'd known...about internet spyware for parents to help monitor a teen's website navigation. Spyware can secretly reveal what sites your children have been visiting and alert you to suspicious activity. One brand of software you might consider is AceSpy and can be purchased at www.acespy.com.

I wish I'd known...to disregard concerns of trust between Ryan and I, and to instead focus on stopping my son from risky behavior. As the parent, it's my job to protect my child until he acquires the common sense that belongs to a mature adult.

After soccer practice at our neighborhood park, I often let the boys play on the playground equipment for a while. An argument always ensued when it was time to go. Ryan would be up on the high bars, or climbing on something else and, rather than come when I called him, I'd have to go get him. Despite losing privileges and serving consequences, Ryan gave me an argument every single time we needed to go home.

One day, in desperation after calling Ryan several times to come get in the car, another family friend, who knew Ryan well, offered to help. The friend's son was playing at the park, too. This clever, trustworthy father told me to leave the park and he'd bring Ryan home. I called Ryan one more time, but Ryan ignored me. So, I accepted the offer of the other parent and went home without saying goodbye to Ryan. It took Ryan a while to discover that he'd been left behind. The other soccer dad kept an eye on Ryan, but let Ryan think he'd been abandoned. When Ryan finally came home, he could not believe I'd left him. However, the next time I called to him that it was time to go home, Ryan came right away. All life lessons for Ryan seemed to be at that same intensity level. Rick and I once read in a magazine that a challenging child was often a very bright child. As Ryan challenged our parenting, I recall Rick looking at me one day and commenting grimly, "I think we have a freakin' genius!"

Rick and I used to tell each other, Ryan was going to do great things if we could keep him on the right track. Ryan was the playground organizer and the other children were attracted to him. He was charismatic, yet bossy, and if others were going to participate, they had to do it exactly as he directed. The children played tag, soccer, "sharks and minnows" in our pool and countless other games. We put up a basketball hoop and the neighborhood kids would play games of "HORSE," "Around the World," and "21." The adults would join the boys and play street hockey. There was always healthy, fun activity at our house. Ryan was a board game real estate tycoon at age 10. He loved the game, Monopoly™, always had to be the banker and, as a result, never lost the game. Rick and I recognized Ryan's leadership as a great trait, but when Ryan was in elementary school, more than once we predicted that the teen years were going to be hard with this child.

Our boys had minimal chores to do each week. They were responsible for keeping their rooms clean, making their beds each day and helping in the kitchen when asked. When he was old enough, Ryan was responsible for mowing our lawn, as well as occasionally pet-sitting or mowing the neighbors' lawns. When Ryan was seven, I was a volunteer with Meals on Wheels, a meal delivery service for senior citizens, and sometimes the boys would tag along with me while I delivered meals. I explained to the boys how delivering a hot meal could brighten the day for lonely, elderly people and how happy these folks often were to see the children. After a nice visit with one of the meal recipients, Ryan commented to me on the way home, "I know we are supposed to do this to make them feel good, but, Mom, it makes me feel good, too."

As our boys grew up, our house was filled with pets. We had a female Dalmatian named Lady when the boys were little. Later we adopted a yellow lab mix named Foxy. Foxy was Rick's dog, but Foxy also loved Ryan because he spent the most time with her. We've always had cats in our house, too. Ryan was always very sensitive and caring with the animals, maybe because he needed the unconditional love they offered him.

THREE

THE WARNING SIGNS OF RYAN'S DRUG USE

When Ryan entered middle school, I began to observe new behaviors. By eighth grade, dedication and determination had been replaced with disrespect and defiance. Ryan's glowing report cards from elementary school were now middle school report cards peppered with lower grades. Since Ryan had always been a challenging child, it was hard for me to distinguish what was "normal" teenage angst and what was potentially something that could be problematic.

I wish I'd known...*poor performance in school doesn't always indicate substance abuse; however, dropping grades often accompany it. This new pattern was a "red flag" that I missed. According to a survey done in 2001 by the National Drug Intelligence Center, the most commonly reported consequence of drug use was poor school performance, truancy, cheating, poor grades, disciplinary problems, expulsion and dropping out.*

I wish I'd known...*students who smoke marijuana get lower grades and are less likely to graduate from high school compared with their non-smoking peers. Depression, anxiety and personality disturbances have been associated with chronic marijuana use. Research has shown that the adverse affects of marijuana impact memory and learning for days or weeks after the acute affects of the drug wear off.*

What Rick and I did know was that Ryan had entered a new phase of his life. What Rick and I didn't know was that Ryan had discovered alcohol in middle school. It wasn't hard to find—we had alcohol in our home. Rick and I weren't "big drinkers," but I liked a glass of red wine and Rick liked a beer now and then. We were responsible, social drinkers, and I thought Rick and I had set good examples for our sons.

> *I wish I'd known*...that alcohol is the most commonly used drug among teenagers. Parents often have a casual attitude about teenage alcohol use. Therefore, teens do not regard alcohol as a dangerous substance. One of the most common places for kids to get their alcohol is from their parents' liquor cabinet or refrigerator.
>
> *I wish I'd known*...according to the results of a recent survey of Pediatrics and Adolescent Medicine, 47% of those who begin drinking alcohol before the age of 14 become alcohol-dependent at some time in their lives, compared with 9% of those who wait until age 21. The correlation holds even when genetic risks for alcoholism are taken into account.
>
> *I wish I'd known*...that alcohol is a factor in the four leading causes of death of among persons ages 10 – 24. (Car accidents, unintentional accidents, homicide, suicide)
>
> *I wish I'd known*...More than 67% of young people who start drinking before the age of 15 will try an illicit drug.

One night, Ryan was hosting a sleepover with several of his friends. I came down the stairs to our family room where the boys were sprawled across the floor in sleeping bags. I heard them whispering, softly giggling, making careful plans about stealing beer from our refrigerator and sneaking out. I sat down on the stairs, stunned, as I listened to the conversation. After I'd heard enough, I stormed into the room, turned on the lights and ended the party. I called all their parents, loaded them into my minivan and took them all home. But I didn't worry too much about it after that. I'd done something similar at that age and, since I'd thwarted the boys' plans, I thought it was a dead issue. I was wrong.

I wish I'd known...*how important it is to be vigilant about preventing your child from sneaking out of the house. An inexpensive security system can alert parents when a teenager is trying to secretly leave the house.*

I wish I'd known...*that sleepovers provide teens with alibis and excellent ways to sneak out; to be somewhere other than where parents think they are and to allow teens unsupervised opportunities to trick parents and find trouble. Even if the sleepover is held at your home, it's wise to do a bed check during the night to confirm that all parties are present and accounted for.*

I wish I'd known...*that friends can place an enormous amount of peer pressure on your teen. One teenager alone can be fairly level-headed, but add one or two teens to the mix and "group pressure" often wins over common sense.*

By age 14 Ryan had graduated to marijuana, but Rick and I still had no idea it was cause for concern. During the summer between eighth grade and high school, Rick and I caught Ryan and his friends in a lie. Ryan and his friend were supposed to be at another friend's home. I called the parents and Ryan wasn't there. Rick and I went out looking for Ryan and when we found him, he and his friends were high on marijuana. Our punishment? Ryan was grounded for two weeks. This was the only time I ever caught Ryan with drugs. I wish I had caught Ryan more than once during those months. Maybe it would have set off an alarm.

I wish I'd known...*having smoked marijuana as a teenager myself during the 1970s, I thought that it was a normal teenage occurrence. But, marijuana today is not the same as it was when I was a kid. I didn't know that. Marijuana today is five times the strength it was in the 1970s and some reports estimate it to be 25 times stronger than earlier decades. Today's marijuana is a totally different, far more dangerous drug.*

Because I had smoked marijuana and used alcohol as a teenager, I didn't think Ryan's behavior was that far out of the ordinary. I had tried it, moved past it and I thought Ryan would, too. I knew teenagers experimented and I thought that when I caught Ryan and grounded him, it was over. I should have used the Action Plan outlined on page 112.

I wish I'd known...more teens are in treatment with a primary diagnosis of marijuana addiction than for all other illicit drugs combined. Not all experimentation will lead to dependency, but it's impossible to predict who will become addicted and who won't. Smoking marijuana leads to changes in the brain that are similar to those caused by cocaine, heroin and alcohol.

After his arrest, Ryan shared with us many of the details of his teen years when he experimented more and more with drugs. According to Ryan, by the middle of his freshman year, he lied to Rick and I all the time. We were unaware of the lies, because by then Ryan had become a talented, proficient liar. He became very good at covering up his deceit. Ryan later told us that, by his sophomore year, his life revolved around homes whose parents were absent and anywhere else he could get high. He told us he hid his drugs well, covering up any evidence of them. He must have, for I never found any of Ryan's drugs.

I wish I'd known...how easy it was for Ryan to hide his marijuana use and the lengths that teens will go to to cover up drug or alcohol use. Please read the warning signs on page 107.

I wish I'd known...how important it is to be awake when your teen comes home in the evening. Give him or her a big hug, and take a deep sniff for tell-tale signs of alcohol or marijuana use. Engage your teen in conversation about the evening to make sure your teen is sober and coherent before going to bed. Teens are awake and talkative late at night and you'll probably find these conversations enlightening and insightful.

I wish I'd known...*teenagers are more sophisticated today than teens of former generations and parents are often shocked to learn of a variety of products known as "stash gear" that are available to assist in hiding drugs. These products are readily available on websites: soda cans with false bottoms to hide drugs; highlighters that actually write on one end and serve as a pipe for marijuana on the other end; and lipsticks built in the same fashion. Teens will often punch a hole through the sheetrock on a wall, and then cover the hole with a poster, to hide drugs. They have been known to hide drugs behind light switch plates and outlet covers in their rooms. They cut pages out of the center of books to hide drugs. The possibilities are endless, as creative teenage minds seek ways to hide drugs. Kids also find creative ways to hide alcohol. They hide their alcohol in sports drink bottles or fast food cups and walk around drinking in public. They usually use vodka because of its lack of odor. For your child's safety and well-being, if you suspect drug or alcohol use, it is imperative to search his or her room for incriminating evidence. Your teenager's life may depend on it. If you find evidence, you must act on it immediately.* See page 107.

How did I miss the smell of pot? Since I experimented with marijuana occasionally as a teenager myself, how did I miss that distinctive odor? After Ryan's arrest, he shared with me that to avoid getting caught, he and his friends would take their shirts off, stand in a straight line, blow the smoke outward, wash their hands, pop some gum, use eye drops, pick up their shirts and come home, eliminating all outward signs of drug use.

FOUR

Ryan's Struggle Affects our Family

I have always been aware of my instincts and my own intuition. Mothers often have natural instincts that develop with our children over time. When my boys were babies, I recall several incidences when one of the boys seemed unusually fussy or a little off. My instincts told me something was wrong, and when I'd take the baby to the doctor, sure enough, there was an ear infection or some other problem the doctor would find. I had learned to trust my instincts about my boys.

A year before Ryan's arrest my gut told me something wasn't right, but I didn't know where or how to look for clues and I thought eventually it would work itself out. I wish I'd listened to that "gut check" and investigated the possibilities more thoroughly. But, I just figured that since Ryan had always made everything so hard, he would have to struggle through it. Believe it or not, until Ryan actually told us he had a drug problem, I truly wasn't thinking of drug addiction.

I wish I'd known...the advantages of drug testing my child. Early intervention can be critical in saving a child from addiction. Because teens lie about drug use, there is no way to verify use without drug testing. Some parents think drug testing violates trust, but teens who are not using drugs have no trust to lose. Kids who have nothing to hide, hide nothing. The safety and well-being of your child must be your first priority.

One of the most powerful reasons to drug test is that it gives teenagers an acceptable excuse to use with their peers when pressured to use drugs. They have the immediate response, "No, my parents drug test me," if or when they are offered drugs. If drug testing confirms your suspicions, you will need a trained drug counselor to determine if your child needs additional help. A great website to visit is www.drugtestyourteen.com for more information.

By midway through his sophomore year, Ryan had become frequently defiant. Rick and I became resigned to this behavior as a defense mechanism to avoid conflict. Our expectations and standards slowly eroded until Ryan's behavior reached a point where he completely crossed the line. We developed an increasing tolerance for his defiance that we would have never accepted earlier in his life. Unless we set out some extreme consequence, Ryan refused to listen to us. We regularly took away his car, grounded him and took away his privileges. Life with Ryan had become a constant battle.

I wish I'd known...about the parenting classes offered by Parent Project®. The curriculum teaches concrete prevention, identification and intervention strategies for the most destructive of adolescent behaviors. (These behaviors include poor school attendance and performance, alcohol and other drug use, gangs, runaways and violent teens.)

One time, during yet another heated argument, Ryan threatened to run away. He said something rude to me and Rick jumped to my defense replying, "No way! You are not going to talk to your mother that way!" Ryan's angry threat was, "I'm out of here." Rick's equally annoyed retort was, "Don't let the door hit you on the way out." I panicked. I told Ryan, "No, you are not going." Then I raced back and forth between Ryan in his room and Rick in his study, trying to repair the damage of the conflict and trying to negotiate peace.

It was at this point that Rick and I each took on the role of a drug addict's parent. Rick was angry, I was worried. As in previous conflicts, Rick and I were at odds with how we should handle Ryan's defiance. This put a strain on our marriage, which added to the stress and turmoil within our family. Frequently, after the issue of the moment had blown over, Rick and I had to repair our relationship. Often I felt angry at Rick for being too hard on Ryan. Then, Rick would be angry with me for not supporting his tough stance. The tension between us was often left unresolved because Ryan's problems would resurface and we were forced to face his issues without enough time or energy to confront our own.

Ryan ended up leaving and it affected our whole family. I was upset for a lot of reasons. I was concerned for Ryan's safety. He was a kid, with nowhere to go. And he was out of control. I didn't realize it then, but it would have been better for Ryan if Rick and I had been on the "same page" in our parenting strategy. Rick was angry at Ryan and wanted Ryan out. I was angry at Rick for not trying to talk the issue through and find a more reasonable solution.

> *I wish I'd known*...*what an emotional toll drug addiction can take on a family and a marriage. Support groups such as Al-Anon can greatly help families. Dealing with a child who has an addiction can make home-life a living hell. Attending a support group is a hard step to take, but may make your struggle easier to bear. Parents who have survived similar situations can be a great comfort to you, as well as a valuable resource. Marriage counseling can help couples separate the issues from their relationship and reinforce the united stand needed when dealing with a drug-addicted family member.*

I have to admit that I was also concerned about what other people in the community would think about my perceived lack of parenting skills. I was a highly visible person in the community. How would this look to the neighbors? I allowed my fear of what others might think about my parenting skills to cloud my judgment about Ryan's threat to run away. It shouldn't have mattered to me what others thought. I should have focused on the best way to help Ryan. My judgment was also hindered because I was fearful that Ryan would become involved in the juvenile justice system or end up with a criminal record.

I wish I'd known...that it is socially acceptable to have a child in crisis and to ask for help. Knowing what I know now, I should have let Ryan run and then called the police to bring him back.

I wish I'd known...that having my son in the juvenile justice system was a far better alternative than a state penitentiary. I also wish I had known... that the juvenile justice system is more about rehabilitation and the adult criminal justice system, where Ryan is now serving his sentence, is more about punishment.

FIVE

RYAN'S DRUG ABUSE IS REVEALED AND TREATMENT BEGINS

L ife with Ryan became constantly chaotic. Ryan would blow up at all sorts of things. Sometimes he seemed to be a loving, charming and normal son. But, I didn't know what was "normal" adolescent behavior and what wasn't. He was always hanging out with friends and had to be constantly doing something. When Ryan was home, he was always tired, sleeping a lot and had trouble getting up for school or work. Even during this turbulent time, he was still sensitive and continued to be the first one to notice if someone else was hurt or sad.

I wish I'd known...sleeping is another red flag for drug abuse. Teenagers require more sleep than adults, but if your teen can't get up for school or work, head's up! Sleeping in on the weekends to do some catching-up is fine, however a teen using drugs will struggle to wake up to attend to basic responsibilities. Mood swings are another symptom parents often overlook with teens in crisis. Overreaction to mild criticism, periods of moodiness, sensitivity, hostility or sudden rage are all symptoms of drug use that parents need to notice. For a full list of signs and symptoms of drug use, see page 107.

During his sophomore year in high school, Ryan told me that he was really sad and thought he might be depressed. This statement was almost a relief because I knew something wasn't right with him. I had a reference point for depression. It was a condition I knew a doctor could treat. I went into my "Mom mode" and dug deeper with lots of pointed questions. "How are you feeling? Are you sad? Are you crying a lot?" Ryan admitted, "Yes, every day." He told me that he didn't feel like doing anything and was completely lacking motivation. I took Ryan to our family doctor who confirmed Ryan's depression and prescribed an antidepressant medication. Ryan said he thought the antidepressant worked for a while and then, after a few months, he thought it wasn't working as well. Our doctor increased the medication dosage. We also enrolled Ryan with a counselor who specialized in adolescent treatment, thinking it would help Ryan navigate some of his extreme emotions. Both professionals missed the real reason behind Ryan's "depression." It was a few months before we all knew the truth. Ryan was mixing marijuana with the antidepressant, Paxil.

I wish I'd known...classic symptoms of depression are also symptoms of marijuana or alcohol abuse. One study shows that students diagnosed with alcohol abuse are more likely to experience major depression than those without the problem.

I wish I'd known...there is a well-known phenomenon called "amotivational syndrome" in which chronic marijuana users become apathetic, socially withdrawn and perform at a level of every day functioning well below their capacity prior to their marijuana use.

I wish I'd known...marijuana has the potential to cause problems in daily life or make a person's existing problems worse. Depression, anxiety and personality disturbances have been associated with chronic marijuana use.

As we sought treatment for Ryan, all of us—parents, counselors and physicians unwittingly deflected attention away from Ryan's actual drug problem. Depression was a smoke screen that prevented us from discovering his reality.

When Ryan was 17, he came into the study where I was working, sat down and confessed that he had a drug problem. He was sobbing and desperate for help. Not realizing the magnitude of the problem, my instant reaction was, "We can handle this. We can fix it." Ryan confessed to smoking a lot of marijuana. We needed help and I went into "Mom Fix It mode" again. "We'll take care of this," I assured Ryan with conviction. Rick and I took Ryan to be assessed at Sierra Family Services in Roseville, California, an out-patient drug treatment facility in our community. Ryan wanted help and we were going to get it for him. The assessment showed that Ryan scored high on the addiction scale and low on the defenses scale. This was concerning to the counselor because this combination frequently indicates a person with suicide tendencies. She suggested that Ryan needed in-patient treatment. I'll never forget Ryan's response at that time when he said, "I'm ready." Immediately I recoiled and thought to myself. "WHAT? We're a good family; we can handle this by ourselves!"

When I found out that in-patient treatment could take up to six months, all I could think of was that Ryan would miss Thanksgiving and Christmas with our family. How ironic and sad to remember that moment now and think of all the Thanksgivings and Christmases he's missed and will continue to miss while serving time in prison. Rick and I opted to begin Ryan in an out-patient treatment program instead of the in-patient program. When I look back now, I realize that when Ryan said, "I'm ready for the in-patient treatment," we should have admitted Ryan right then and there. The out-patient treatment wasn't an effective tool because Ryan's window of accepting treatment and admitting that he needed help slammed shut soon after.

I wish I'd known...*a drug addict's willingness to get help can be a very brief, fleeting moment. When Ryan told me he was ready to seek in-patient treatment, I might have prevented his self-destruction if I had agreed to send him immediately.*

I wish I'd known...*most compulsive drug users can't quit on their own, even if they want to. Teens who are addicted to drugs may be fearful about treatment, so starting treatment when teenagers are ready is critical to success. Treatment does not need to be voluntary to be effective. Parents can provide strong motivation.*

I wish I'd known...*treating teenagers early can save their lives. Because adolescent brains and bodies are not fully developed, dependency can progress rapidly. Other factors include teenagers' tendency to use a variety of substances all at once, and in an environment where the purpose of using drugs is for intoxication.*

One day I observed another glimpse into the depth of Ryan's problem. He was lying on the floor in the family room and we were having a heart to heart talk about life in general. "What do you want to do with the rest of your life?" I asked him. I was stunned as he replied, "Mom, all I want to do is get high and listen to music." He was serious. I was shocked. I counseled him, "Ryan, that's not life, we've got to get you some other kind of help."

I started researching other treatment places. I found the New Dawn Recovery Center, which offered intense out-patient treatment Monday through Friday. Our medical insurance would cover it and Ryan was willing to go. At New Dawn, Ryan was assessed by Michael Moncrieff, an adolescent drug counselor and, for the first time, I felt that we had somebody finally fighting with us. But, I was still ignorant of the incredible odds we were facing to save our son. As Ryan continued to battle drug addiction, he was losing ground. Rick and I had no idea where to turn. We had no one to talk to who understood Ryan's problem and we felt very isolated. We were hesitant to talk about the problem with our friends because we were embarrassed and ashamed of Ryan, his problem and our apparent failure as parents.

I wish I'd known...*other parents who had faced this problem before me. It wasn't a topic discussed in our community. When Ryan was arrested and I was forced to face this publicly, people began to share their own personal family problems, criminal past or drug addiction. I had become somebody who was safe to talk to. People seemed to sense that I wouldn't judge them, since my situation was so dire.*

Ryan continued to attend out-patient treatment Monday through Friday. He participated successfully for two weeks and then Ryan brought alcohol to the group in a fast food cup. He shared it with others during a break in the group therapy session. At that point the counselor, Michael, became alarmed. He called us and recommended that Ryan receive in-patient treatment. This time I agreed. I knew what we were doing wasn't working and, despite missing Ryan from our family, I knew that we needed to send him away for treatment. I told Michael, "I don't think he'll go willingly." I had visions of a huge confrontation with Ryan if I suggested he begin in-patient care. I was deeply afraid of the potential scene and I thought Ryan would just take off, run away and become even more dependent on drugs.

Michael agreed with me. He told us not to tell Ryan what we were planning. We crafted a plan to pack some clothes for Ryan and pretend to take him for an appointment with a doctor who specialized in drug addiction. I didn't sleep a wink the night before because I was consumed with anxiety. I never lied to my children, and this was such a manipulative, deceitful plan, I feared that it might totally alienate Ryan from us. He was not going to want to go and he would hate us for sending him there. But I knew we were out of options.

I wish I'd known...most compulsive drug users cannot stop using on their own, even if they want to. This is why forced drug treatment becomes necessary. Denial is a defense mechanism and is an integral part of the disease. Typically an alcoholic or an addict is the last to admit he has a problem. In an effort to keep your teen from hitting a "bottom" or low-point that may be life-damaging, you can enforce very strict rules and consequences for your drug-addicted teenager, such as curfews, ultimatums and the removal of privileges (the use of a car, cell phone, computer, etc.) When your teen's drug use becomes the most important thing in the world to him or her, the most prudent course of action may be placement in a residential drug treatment program.

Rick, Ryan and I were headed for Camp Recovery Center in Santa Cruz, California, about 150 miles west of our home. It didn't take Ryan long to figure out that we weren't going to the doctor. We were heading down the freeway, beyond the normal exit where we would turn off for the doctor's office, when Ryan looked behind the seat in our Chevy Blazer to find his sports bag. "What the hell are my clothes doing in the back?" Ryan demanded. Rick said, "We're taking you to in-patient drug treatment." Ryan's face told me he was incredulous. And yet, there was a look that showed he was also halfway impressed. Ryan could not believe we'd managed to dupe him. Then, he began seething with anger. My heart was racing with fear and I had visions of Ryan jumping out of the car on the freeway or running away at a gas stop.

When we arrived at the treatment facility, the staff was prepared and waiting for us. They took Ryan and did an assessment to see if he was qualified for their program. They interviewed Rick and I and asked us countless questions. When it was time to go, we told Ryan we loved him. As we were pulling out of the driveway, I looked back to see Ryan sitting on a bench looking like a scared little boy. What was ahead? Everything in me wanted to stop the car and go back and get him. But deep down I knew that Ryan had a serious problem. The look on Ryan's face told me that he was baffled that we would abandon him. I cried all the way home. My heart was broken and I felt that I actually had abandoned Ryan.

> *I wish I'd known...that sometimes the hardest thing you have to do as a parent is also the most loving thing you can do.*

I thought that during the first night we'd get a phone call that Ryan had run away from the treatment center. This was not a "lock down" facility. There were no bars on the windows or locks on the doors. We took him on a Wednesday and there was a mandatory parent day three days later on Saturday. There were no phone calls allowed. I'll never forget the first parent day Rick and I attended, because, on this day, I began my education in drug addiction. This was the first time I really received concrete, clinical information regarding Ryan's drug addiction. Rick and I started the session by listening to a recovered addict tell his story of alcohol addiction and relapse after eight years of sobriety. His relapse started with just a single one-ounce bottle of bourbon consumed during an airplane ride. He told us that he woke up in the hospital with all his front teeth broken less than

24 hours after that single drink. I was shocked to hear that a one-ounce bottle of alcohol had reawakened his addiction after eight years of sobriety. It was the first time I realized that Ryan was facing a lifetime disease. It was incredibly discouraging! It was hard to accept that relapse would be part of Ryan's recovery. The statistics the speaker gave us for addicted adolescents were dismal at best. He told us that 3 out of 20 addicted teenagers make it to their 25th birthday without being dead, incarcerated or hospitalized. That was when Rick and I first realized the severity of what lay ahead.

For part of that day, the center staff had us break up into groups and instructed us to talk to another child who was in treatment. Ryan talked to another parent while we talked to another patient out in the yard. This was eye-opening for me and a good activity because I was able to ask questions without personal emotions getting in the way. Both Rick and I were able to really hear what the drug-addicted child was saying. The boy that we were talking to was such a good-hearted kid and he felt extremely bad about what he'd put his family through. I think this conversation helped me see that Ryan, the person I knew and loved, was still in there, somewhere. It gave me a whisper of hope.

> *I wish I'd known...prior to Ryan's illness, I tended to characterize people who took drugs as morally weak. I felt they could just stop using drugs if they wanted to badly enough. Overcoming these myths with scientific knowledge helped me understand the problem of addiction. Part of the difficulty in treating drug addiction is the stigma associated with the disease.*

When we talked to Ryan that day, he was still angry with us, but in a less intense way. Rick and I told him we loved him and felt better about our decision to leave him at the treatment center. I actually felt better and worse that day. I felt better because we were getting him the help he needed and I also felt that we had hope for the first time. I felt worse because I saw the road ahead was going to be very treacherous, tedious and tiring. While it was going to be a long recovery, I knew Ryan was in the right place for treatment.

During the following days, I tried to get some rest because I knew I'd need to be ready to support Ryan's battle when he came home. I was resting up to fight his drug addiction with all I had to give. It was during this time that I began to think that it would have been easier if Ryan had suffered from a serious illness such as cancer rather than drug addiction. Cancer victims want help, seek help and willingly follow treatment and protocol. Drug addicts rarely admit they have a disease and seldom want help to get better. It's easy to find doctors and treatment facilities for cancer patients. Drug addiction treatment facilities for adolescents are hard to find and are extremely impacted. More than once I didn't know what to do or where to take Ryan for help. I was embarrassed to talk about Ryan's problems and felt that I'd failed as a parent. If Ryan had been diagnosed with cancer, the guilt and embarrassment wouldn't have been an issue and a plan of action or protocol would have been readily available.

I initially thought Ryan would be at the in-patient treatment center in Santa Cruz for 30 days. But just 4 days after that first parent day, Ryan and 2 other teen patients tried to break into the medicine cabinet in the nurse's office. Their plan was to steal cold medicine to get high. The center immediately discharged him. He was kicked out of the treatment program for violating the rules of the center and the code of rehabilitation. We received a phone call and were told to come and pick Ryan up immediately. This was the second worst day of my life. Devastated, Rick and I looked at each other in despair and asked, "Now what do we do?" We had absolutely no idea of what to do with Ryan. We were tossed into a black, stormy sea with no hope or direction. It was horrible.

The return trip from Santa Cruz included an assessment at Catholic West Hospital. I was grasping at straws at that point. There was a possibility that Catholic West would admit Ryan if he posed a risk to himself or others. But, that assessment told us that Ryan did not have other mental health issues, such as bipolar tendencies, suicide ideations or severe depression. Their assessment revealed that all of Ryan's problems simply stemmed from drug addiction. As we neared home, Ryan told us that the combination of being admitted to the in-patient treatment center and getting kicked out of it were the first real consequences of his drug use. These two events woke

Ryan up to the realization that he did indeed have a problem with drug addiction. Prior to this, Ryan had never been penalized or inconvenienced for his drug use. Ryan had lived a lifestyle of drug abuse and had gotten away with it for years without negative consequences!

> *I wish I'd known...risky behaviors can be symptoms of drug abuse. It struck me then, that a year earlier, Ryan had received a ticket for reckless driving. I hadn't yet linked this risky behavior with drug addiction, but the pieces of the puzzle were slowly coming together.*

In the car, with a soft sigh, Ryan said to us in a very quiet, resigned voice, "That's where I needed to be." Rick and I were astonished. We thought he might come back belligerent and still angry. But Ryan was very distraught, penitent and sad. Once again the window of wanting treatment was opened. Ryan told Rick and I that he couldn't believe the in-patient recovery center was kicking him out. In that week he learned enough to know he needed serious treatment. But despite our pleadings, the recovery center would not take him back. In desperation, I called Michael Moncrieff, the counselor from New Dawn, for some direction on what to do with our unstable son. There was no choice but to bring him home. Michael's advice scared me. He told me to lock up everything. This included non-prescription cold medicine, prescriptions, jewelry, wallets, anything of value, including any weapons such as guns or knives. This was even more terrifying. We didn't own any weapons. There were no guns or hunting equipment at our home. Why would that even be a consideration? "Batten down the house," was his advice. "I don't know if they'll let him back in at New Dawn," Michael advised us. But, he promised to advocate for Ryan.

SIX

67 Days of Sobriety

Michael persuaded the New Dawn Recovery Center to accept Ryan back into the program again with the condition that Ryan sign a contract and strictly adhere to the rules of the program. This began the start of Ryan's 67 days of sobriety. Every day of sobriety is celebrated and tallied by addicts in recovery. Ryan began to spill all his secrets to Rick and I while he went to Alcoholics Anonymous and Narcotics Anonymous meetings once or twice a day. He began to share just how deeply embedded with drugs his life had been in our community. Ryan threw himself into his sobriety with the same intensity as he had thrown himself into his addiction. He was determined to stay clean and sober. "It feels so good," Ryan told us about not lying anymore. During Ryan's 67 days of sobriety he told us, "I love you so much and you guys are my reason for staying sober and clean. I don't want to hurt you anymore." These words filled me with hope and yet… there was still a pit of fear in my stomach about what was ahead for us. There was that word called "relapse," an event we were told happens often on a person's path toward final recovery. It was a word that filled me with dread.

During this period, Rick and I were stunned at Ryan's account of how many kids in our community were using drugs, how many types of drugs were being used and how easy drugs were to get. Drugs had invaded our community in mind-blowing proportions. Rick and I had no idea there were drugs available to our city's children and we were pretty sure nobody else in our community knew about this extensive drug usage, either. Yet, while we felt others needed to know this, we really didn't do anything with that information at the time. Our first priority was trying to keep Ryan safe and sober.

> *I wish I'd known*...*drugs do not just reside in inner cities and gang areas. Drugs are a real problem in every community, and affects society with increased crime, violence, teen pregnancy, AIDS and countless other ills. Drug abuse is a national public crisis with wide-ranging social consequences.*

It took me awhile to realize that it didn't matter anymore what Rick and I wanted for Ryan. It really came down to the fact that we could do nothing. It had to be Ryan's decision to stay off drugs. There was no peace with this realization. From the first day of Ryan's sobriety until his arrest, I had a constant anticipation of dread in my stomach. I knew the statistics and that the chance of a relapse was very high. I didn't know what it would bring, but I knew it wouldn't be good. I don't know if it was a mother's premonition that something much graver was ahead, but I was waiting for that "other shoe to drop." The fear inside me was something I handed over to God, again and again and again. I knew God had a plan for Ryan's life, but I didn't know if I could endure it.

Ryan continued in New Dawn out-patient treatment and AA meetings. Again, unbeknownst to Rick and me, Ryan steered off the path of sobriety 67 days later on New Years Eve, when he drank alcohol as part of a celebration. Ryan told us after his arrest that he felt really bad about that relapse and actually abstained from alcohol or drugs for another week. But, within ten days of New Years Eve, the alcohol and drugs had again invaded Ryan's life. As part of our treatment support for Ryan's sobriety, Rick and I randomly drug tested Ryan, using alcohol swabs and drug testing kits. No alcohol or drugs showed up during our testing, as Ryan creatively "beat the tests." By mid-January Ryan was back in his cycle of addiction. He told us later that he was, "full blown doing 'my thing' (using drugs) from mid-January to March, on a 24/7 high."

> *I wish I'd known*...on the internet there are entire websites devoted to the topic of how to beat drug tests. Addicted teens will go to great lengths to foil a drug test. Teens have been known to substitute another person's clean urine, or add substances to their own urine to beat a test. They also take large doses of detoxification supplements to block the detection of drugs in their systems.

Ryan told us later that during those days, he'd use anything he could get his hands on to get high. He was using cocaine, pills, mushrooms, Vicodin, Valium, Percoset, Adderall and Dilaudid. He freebased, smoked heroin, tried methamphetamines, and then dropped everything except Coricidin (an over-the-counter cold medicine) and marijuana.

> *I wish I'd known*...about the dangers common household medicine cabinets hold for teenagers. Today's teens are more likely to abuse prescription and over-the-counter medications than illegal drugs because they think it's "safer." However, when cold medicines or pain killers are abused and not taken for their prescribed use, these medications can become as dangerous as illegal drugs. Cough medicine is often combined with other substances, which can increase the dangerous side affects.

During this time we were not giving Ryan money to support his drug habits and he had only a part-time job at a retail store. But, Ryan found other ways to support his drug needs and used his ingenuity to steal from a variety of places. Once, Ryan was accused of stealing money from the high school locker room. The assistant principal called and asked me to have Ryan come in for questioning. I listened to the charges and promised to send him to the school, but I assured the administrator that Ryan would never steal. I was still unaware of Ryan's desperate measures to fund his drug habit. Later I learned that Ryan had stolen from the school locker room many times. Ryan also borrowed money from many people, never intending to pay it back. He did not ever steal any of our family valuables or my jewelry, but after his arrest he admitted to taking money from our wallets. Supporting a drug habit is expensive and Ryan found creative ways to fund his habit.

> *I wish I'd known...how desperate a person can get to find drugs and how powerful the pull of drugs can become. Despite the best intentions and will power, the magnetism of drugs supercedes all values and morals for an addict. For these reasons, drug addiction and alcoholism are said to be cunning diseases. Once, while talking to a recovering addict, he explained to me that if his own mother was between him and his drug, he would have run over his mother to get to the drug. Wow!*

Incredibly, during this time, Ryan seemed to be doing well in his fight with drug addiction. I didn't notice anything amiss, but the sense of unease was still present. Knowing that relapse was a real possibility, one day I sat him down on a patio chair in the back yard and just asked, "Ryan, how are you doing in your fight with drugs? Are you struggling? Are you having a hard time with it?" I was looking for hints of relapse or signs that things weren't going well. I still recall with crystal clarity Ryan looking me straight in the eye, and answering sweetly, "Really good, Mom. I'm just fine." I pressed him, "Are you using drugs again?" And again, right into my eyes, he answered, "No Mom, I'm just fine." I believed him. Drug addicts lie so well.

> *I wish I'd known...effective drug testing can uncover lies. If possible, when administering a drug test, a same-sex parent should be present when the specimen is taken and a thermometer should verify the body temperature of the sample. Do not tell your teen in advance of a drug test. A true sample should be taken randomly, with no advance warning.*

One of the things I learned in drug counseling was not to be an "enabler." But, as a mother, I am an enabler. That's part of my job. I took good care of my kids. How could I stop helping my son? How could I just stop being his mother? The counselor told me that I had to figure out how to detach myself from Ryan and his problem. As a mother, that went against everything I believed in and had practiced for 18 years. In the beginning, I couldn't separate the disease from Ryan. But I came to understand that Ryan had to make the decision himself not to use drugs. Here I had a child with a huge problem that could kill him and I was supposed to cut all strings and let him figure it out? I had to learn that it was Ryan's decision and, as much as I wanted it for him, it was his choice and his choice alone. How could I do that? I'd helped him do all things in his life. In the words of the counselor, "If Ryan chooses to go back and use drugs, there is nothing on this planet you can do to stop him." What? How could this be? I couldn't comprehend that statement. But I had to. I had to get there to save my sanity.

> ***I wish I'd known****...the alienating behavior of a teenage drug addict obscures the love he feels for his parents. Parents are not struggling with their teenager, the fight is with the teen's compulsion to use drugs. When using drugs hits the top of your adolescent's priority list, it doesn't change the fact that the teen loves you as his parent, it's just that drugs trump everything, including family.*

Two days before his arrest, Ryan came to Rick and I again and told us he had started using drugs. I think I was expecting this on some level. It was exactly what the drug counselors had told us to expect. But, Ryan was now 18 and we no longer had control to force Ryan into treatment. This was a new wrinkle in the plan. We'd been educated on how to handle this. Rick and I had zero tolerance for drug use in our home, but we were committed to helping Ryan find help. Right away, I started calling treatment facilities, looking for nearby places with an opening for Ryan. I located two options for treatment. Rick and I gave Ryan the names of two different places that agreed to admit him and we begged Ryan to seek treatment before something dreadful happened. We even printed the directions on how to drive there, and offered to take him ourselves. At this point, I wasn't shocked. I was resigned. I told Ryan. "We knew this was a possibility, but you have to get help." Rick told him, "I love you and want the very best for you, but you can't stay at our house if you're using drugs. You cannot jeopardize the rest of our family." Ryan went up to his room and came down the stairs with a packed bag. He told us, "I have some thinking to do." As he was leaving, I was terrified that I might never see him again. I was so afraid that he'd suffer a drug overdose or get into a car accident. Rick and I encouraged him one more time to check himself in for treatment. We told him we loved him as he walked out the door.

The next day, a jittery, nervous Ryan came home. When we first saw him, we were hopeful that he'd changed his mind and was ready for treatment. He didn't stay long, but he was obviously edgy and "amped up." This was the first time I ever recognized Ryan visibly altered and under the influence of drugs. Ryan had always gone to great lengths to keep his drug use a secret from us. This time he made no effort to hide it. "Did you change your mind?" I asked hopefully. "No, just getting more clothes," was his reply.

What Rick and I didn't know was that, just before his return, Ryan had acquired a .22 caliber handgun from a friend and, along with another juvenile friend, had begun a crime spree along the interstate freeway near our home. Ryan had just committed armed robbery at a gas station, a convenience store and a grocery store not 30 miles from our house. After he was arrested, Ryan admitted to me that he had just come home that last day to steal from us. His plan was to take jewelry, our ATM cards or money. But he had a moment of conscience and only took a small amount of cash that day.

As Ryan went out the door this last time, I had this terrible sense of dread. My mother's instincts were screaming that Ryan was in deep trouble and things were going to go from bad to worse. It was the last time I saw Ryan in the free world.

I wished I'd known…

Ryan left our house, picked up two 17-year-old males and left. He then held up a second gas station and a bookstore at knifepoint before he was arrested by Nevada County deputies in Truckee, California, a small town at the summit of Donner Pass in the Sierra Nevada Mountains. Ryan was charged with multiple counts of armed robbery and, because he was 18 and his companions in crime were all minors, he was considered the adult contributing to the delinquency of these minors.

When Ryan left our house that last time, I also left to go on an overnight getaway with my mother and sister. I'd lost my enthusiasm for going because of Ryan's situation, but this trip had been planned in advance and Rick encouraged me to go. My mom had made reservations to stay overnight at a bed and breakfast in Nevada City, a quaint historical gold rush city in the Sierra foothills. We were going to do a bit of shopping. Throughout the day, my mind kept wandering back to Ryan, whispering prayers for his safety. I knew that wherever Ryan was headed, it wasn't good. I was finally facing the fact that my son was a drug addict and out of control. Shopping just wasn't important that day. Early Sunday morning I asked to go home. Ironically, I left Nevada City around 10 a.m., only to find out later that Ryan had been booked earlier that same morning in Nevada City in the Nevada County Jail.

SEVEN

THE ROAD TO RYAN'S VICTORY

The Monday after Ryan's arrest, Justin, at age 15, elected to go to school. This was the same school that Ryan had attended and where everyone would be talking about Ryan. I was astounded at Justin's determination to go on with his life and face what was ahead with such courage. It couldn't have been easy for him to face a campus with over 2,000 students and 150 staff members. But Justin didn't miss a beat. He went to school, went to baseball practice, worked on his homework and kept up his athletic workouts. However, Justin suffered later as the bottled-up stress internally attacked his immune system. He became ill with a variety of viruses, infections and other ailments during the next four months. Justin proved to be resilient, but he wasn't "superman."

After Ryan's arrest and conviction, I suffered extreme anxiety about going out in public. Ryan's arrest had been on the front page of our local newspaper and was aired on our local television station during the news hour. I didn't want to use my credit card because it had my name on it and someone might link what Ryan did to me. I was embarrassed to be associated with Ryan's name. I entered counseling and my counselor pushed me to answer the question, "What's the worst thing that can happen?" I realized that my fears were of a public judgment or pity and how I might break down in tears or collapse in public. I was concerned that someone would ask me pointed questions like, "Why didn't you…?" or "How could you let this happen?"

Just the thought of going into the grocery store had become an anxiety-producing event. I was afraid that I might run into someone familiar. And I worried about what that person might be thinking of me or my family. The first weeks after Ryan's arrest, Rick and I drove to Folsom, a small town about 20 miles from our home, just to go out to dinner, hoping we were far enough away from Rocklin to avoid the notoriety.

Slowly, over time, I figured out that nobody has that perfect family and it became very liberating to not worry about what other people might think or say. I held on to the fact that the people who knew me and watched me mother my children knew the truth. Those who had ill thoughts or were judgmental became unimportant. That was a huge paradigm shift for my mind. Once I got over the shock of Ryan's crimes and subsequent arrest, I felt a peace about his situation. It was as if I had been holding my breath underwater and I suddenly surfaced to gasp a breath of fresh air. It wasn't a peace that things were "over." However, I felt better because at least now I knew where Ryan was. The turmoil in our house ceased when Ryan was arrested.

As sad as it sounds, things were better for Rick, Justin and I without Ryan in our home. I felt very guilty about that for a long time. But, it truly was more peaceful at home. Rick, Justin and I all felt it, but nobody wanted to say it out loud, thinking it would seem as if we didn't miss Ryan. We missed Ryan, but we did not miss the stress and chaos that Ryan brought with him.

Ryan spent two months in Nevada County and then was transferred to Placer County Jail, where he spent the next 10 months. Phone calls were recorded, making it impossible for us to learn any of the details of the crimes from Ryan. Visits were occasional and monitored behind glass, so it was a full year before we got to hold Ryan, embrace him or hug him. It was a full year before we could talk to him without the conversation being recorded. Ryan's criminal charges included five counts of armed robbery. The law considered him an adult; a man. To me, he was still a boy and I didn't think he should be housed with seasoned criminals.

A plea bargain was arranged between the defense attorney and prosecutor. The bargain consisted of 10 years of mandatory prison for using a gun in the crime, 18 months for robbery with a weapon, and 18 months for an additional robbery. This totaled 13 years. The 13 year sentence could be reduced to 85 percent of that total time if Ryan would serve his sentence "on good behavior." This meant Ryan could be paroled after serving 11 years. While this seemed harsh, California law could have dictated that Ryan received 65 years for his crimes. Ryan will be 29 years old if he's released after serving 85% of his sentence; 31 if he serves the full 13 years.

Ryan was eventually transferred to a maximum security California State Penitentiary where he now lives in a 5-foot by 8-foot cell 23 hours a day. As a prison inmate, Ryan does not use drugs. He has become a voracious reader, is taking correspondence college courses and hopes to have his Bachelor's Degree before he is released. Ryan's main goal in prison is to "stay out of the fray." He has renewed his faith in God and hopes to one day become a drug and alcohol rehabilitation counselor. A family friend has offered Ryan a job in construction when he is paroled. His current plans are to simply remain clean and sober, be content and stay strong. He chooses to make the time that he serves in prison count for something.

As Ryan was able to talk to us from prison, Rick and I began to see just how little we knew about drugs and what drug addiction does to teenagers. Ryan was not eager to go back to his past and he's shameful of the life he lived which led to his arrest and conviction. But, glimpses of his drug addictive lifestyle were startling from his perspective! I began to research drug addiction and soon learned an enormous amount of information that could save lives; lives of children, as well as those who love their children.

Today, I feel that Ryan's incarceration is easier for him than living as a drug addict. Ryan told us shortly after he was arrested that, if he hadn't been arrested, he'd be dead. As he has revealed to us over the past months the extent to which he was using drugs prior to his arrest, I know he is probably right. Now, with Ryan in prison, I know where he is. As brutal as it sounds to be glad my son is in a maximum security prison, I'm happy to say that Ryan is doing well there. He's beating his addiction and he's matured into a man of whom I can be proud. I'm pleased with how he handles himself and his new goals.

The first days after Ryan's crime spree, I truly felt that it would have been better if he had died, rather than face his dark and desperate future. Because the Ryan that I gave birth to, nurtured and loved had died. He was gone. But, my Ryan has been reborn. Today he's clean, sober, clear-headed, focused and motivated. The changes I see in him inspire me to believe that prison has saved our son. Ryan is no longer a drug-addicted stranger. Rick and I have our son back. Each time I go to visit him in prison it reminds me to be thankful that I'm not visiting his graveside. Ryan has accepted his sentence and his situation. He's been stripped of everything and his true character has been revealed. At the base of who Ryan is, he has kept a positive outlook. He has accepted full responsibility for all his crimes and has tried to make the best of his punishment. Ryan has renewed his faith in God.

Folsom Lake, 1992

Christy & Ryan, 1986

December 1985

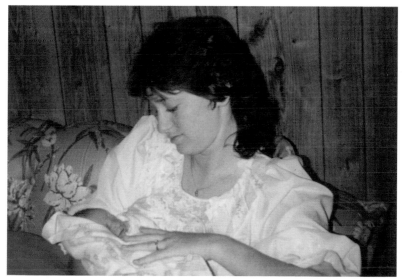

First Day Home from Hospital with Ryan

Christmas 2002

Crandell Family, Folsom State Prison, 2006

In front of our soon-to-be new home, 2001

Christmas 2002

A bike ride with Dad, 1993

Ryan with his cousin, Danny

Family Cruise, 2001

4th of July in Grants Pass, Oregon

Easter on Milburn Street

1st Day of School on Milburn Street

Tree swing in Oregon, age four

Ryan, age two

Ryan & Christy, Maui, 2002

Rick & Ryan, Father's Day, Folsom State Prison 2006

Ryan with his best friend, Erik

Ryan & Foxy

Ryan & Justin, 1999

*Ryan & Justin
in Catalina*

*Ryan & Justin, Solano Prison
in Vacaville, 2004*

Christmas 1995

Halloween 1992

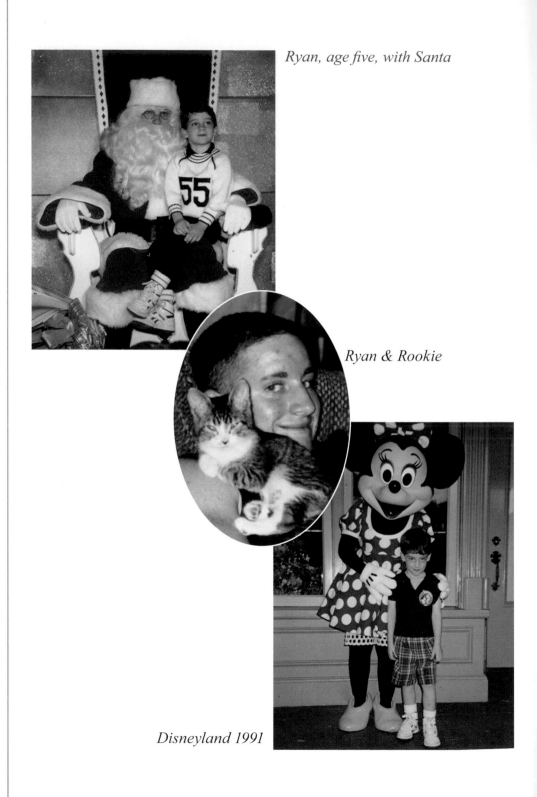

Ryan, age five, with Santa

Ryan & Rookie

Disneyland 1991

Little Thunder Basketball 1996

Ryan, age 17

Junior Varsity Football

*Ryan with mask,
cape and sword, age four*

Ryan, age 18 months

Halloween 1997

Ryan & Justin 1996

*Helping his brother
with homework*

Watching Justin's soccer game

Happy 9th Birthday

Maui 2002

Ryan with his PaPa and GiGi,
Folsom State Prison, 2005

Ryan with his aunt, uncle and cousins,
Folsom State Prison, 2006

Ryan with his grandparents,
Folsom State Prison, 2006

EIGHT

ON GUARD: IT WON'T HAPPEN ON MY WATCH!

When Ryan was arrested, I felt that it was all too much to bear. And yet, I have. It wasn't easy, but I did it. And I am now determined to do everything I can to prevent other children from falling prey to the same demons, the same destruction and the same devastation as did Ryan. Today, I work as a facilitator for Parent Project®, a nationally recognized parent training program designed specifically for parents of strong-willed or out-of-control adolescent children. I strive to help families dealing with the ravages of drug abuse. I am an advocate for parents of teens in crisis and do my best to provide information and support for families who are dealing with issues involving substance abuse. Some time ago, Rick and I gathered like-minded parents in our community and called ourselves Rocklin Community Against Substance Abuse (RCASA). We've effectively made changes and raised awareness regarding this issue in our community, offering services such as an anonymous hotline to report drug and alcohol activity. Although my initial goal was to reach our community, I recently launched a national website dedicated to informing parents around the country about the dangers of teenage drug abuse, www.stopteendrugaddiction.com, and I plan to expand my speaking schedule to include audiences around the country.

I am passionately active with local teens, offering information without judgment and encouraging them to examine risky behaviors before trouble overtakes them. I have developed a wealth of resources for parents and teens when they are finally ready for help. I receive phone calls several times a month and sometimes several per week from hopeless and scared parents seeking support and resources for their teens in crisis. It makes me feel good to help them and this has helped with my own healing process. There have been many positive things that have come out of Ryan's ordeal. Families in our community were impacted when Ryan was arrested. Because of the publicity and the fact that Rick and I were so visible in the community, it was clear that this kind of thing could indeed happen to families like ours. People have told me that they saw our entire community affected by this tragedy. Parents were jolted into talking to their kids about drugs that week.

I'm told that many kids in our community have changed their paths as a result of Ryan's ordeal. Many of Ryan's friends were in court when he was sentenced to serve 13 years in the California State Penitentiary for his crime. Today, I never hesitate to lend unsolicited counsel to kids within my sphere of influence, especially to those whom I know and care about. I'm on guard for their well-being. These teenagers know that if I hear anything amiss, I'll hunt them down and make sure they get the help they need before it's too late. I'm not going to stand by and watch another child I care about go down the path to destruction. It's not going to happen on my watch!

When Ryan was in his third year of prison, he put his experiences with drug addiction in a journal. After I read these writings, I was amazed at how I missed all the signs of Ryan's drug use. I thought at first that I must have been an incompetent parent. I never imagined the amount of drugs Ryan was doing or how much time he spent being high. Reading his journal brought me back to such a level of despair, I don't know how I lived through it. When I'm working now with other families, I identify with their despair and try to offer them hope and understanding without judgment. Was Ryan's problem major denial on our part? Was it ignorance? Was it fear? Looking back, it was probably all three. I still ask myself why. Why him? Why us? Why such a tough lesson? Then I remind myself of all the blessings that have come from this tragedy and I thank God for being able to help others avoid the same calamity our family suffered.

Even in the darkest moments of Ryan's battle with drug addiction, I had a strong sense that our family was being called to do something with this tragedy. It was just a small flicker of hope. It took a lot of courage, prayer and determination, but now, with guidance, encouragement and perspective from Ryan, Rick and I are dedicated to making a difference in the fight against drugs in our world.

NINE

FROM THE EYES OF RYAN'S FATHER

The morning Ryan was arrested, I woke up alone. The phone was ringing at 4 a.m. and Christy was gone with her sister and mother on an outing. The phone kept ringing and I dragged myself awake to hear a person identify himself as a detective from the Nevada County Sheriff's Office. He asked me if I had a son named Ryan Crandell. I was still half asleep, but I answered, "Yes." The detective gravely explained that he had my son in custody for multiple crimes of armed robbery and that he had a few questions for me. I heard his words, but what he meant was still a little fuzzy. I was trying to wake up, but the nightmare was just getting started. I told the detective that I would need to call him back. I got up, washed my face, gathered my courage and returned the call. The detective explained that over the last two days, Ryan and three other teens had gone on a robbery spree from Placer to Nevada counties. Only a few hours earlier, Ryan had robbed a bookstore where he'd held the clerk at knifepoint. After a high speed chase in Truckee, Ryan was captured, caught with the money from the bookstore robbery and was now incarcerated along with three other boys.

The detective wanted to know what I knew about Ryan's activities. I told him that Ryan had been struggling with drug use and abuse for several months; that he'd been in rehab and doing very well. I told him that about a week prior, when we had realized Ryan was using drugs again, I had told Ryan that he couldn't continue living in our home if he was using drugs.

I told the officer that I had seen Ryan as recently as the day before, just briefly when Christy and I had encouraged him to get help. We'd given him telephone numbers of rehab centers and offered to take him, but Ryan had refused our offers of help. I explained that Ryan had taken the phone numbers and told us he had some things to think about. While in this conversation, I was trying to remain calm and collected. But my initial response was terror for my son. Here was a mixed-up kid that I loved more than life—in jail. I was sure he was scared. All I could think about was how can I help him? How can I get him out? As his dad, what can I do here? What was my best move? I didn't know anything about criminal law. But, based on the officer's shared information about the crimes—multiple robberies, a gun and a knife, I knew Ryan was in very serious trouble.

I hung up the phone and tried to wake up, clear my mind and formulate a plan of action to help Ryan. There was no one to talk to at that hour with Christy away. I was just sitting there, trying to figure out what I could do. When our younger son, Justin, who was 15 at the time, got up for church, I briefly explained that Ryan had been arrested and we didn't know for sure all that had transpired. I didn't know what to do beyond that so Justin and I went to church. There I met our friend and neighbor and told her what had happened. I was kind of in a fog. I didn't know what to do at that point. In my mind, I was thinking that somehow there must be a way for me to help my son. While I fought off panic and paralyzing fear, I kept thinking, "There's got to be a way." I needed to understand the scope and magnitude of what had transpired. And, I didn't know how I was going to explain this to Christy. As the church service closed, I realized that Christy would soon be home from her trip. I knew she would take this hard. I was then dismayed to learn that Christy had actually come home earlier than I had anticipated. She'd seen a call from the Nevada County Sheriff's Department on our telephone identification list. And, by the time I walked in the door, she was pale with worry.

In the presence of Christy's mother, sister and Justin, I shared the details of what I knew had happened. Then my world crumbled before my eyes as Christy completely collapsed. She fell, wailing on the floor. Her sobs gripped my heart and, as much as I shared her grief, I was unable to console her. The whole situation was surreal. As Ryan's father, I was sitting in my living room with my wife on the floor, sobbing out of control, unable to do anything to help my son or my wife. I felt helpless. I couldn't do anything to help or save my son, my wife was falling apart, my youngest son was witnessing this tragedy and I had to drag myself into the realization that we were experiencing real time here. It was overwhelming. I was able to keep myself together by taking an analytical approach. My focus became, "What do we do from here?" I had already retained a lawyer to protect Ryan's rights. So, what would come next?

As I spoke with Ryan's lawyer and court officials, I was shocked at the sentence Ryan was facing. California law dictated that Ryan could be sentenced to state prison for up to 65 years for his crimes. In trying to work through all of this chaos, my goal and my mission became to do everything humanly possible to get Ryan's sentence reduced. I didn't believe that 65 years of prison fit the crime at all. Prior to this event, Ryan had never been in trouble with the law, he was just three weeks past his 18th birthday, and to me, he was still just a mixed-up kid. Sixty-five years in the state pen? Where was the justice in that? The day Ryan was sentenced, the courtroom was overflowing with family, friends, classmates, neighborhood kids and even teachers who loved and supported Ryan. Before the judge pronounced Ryan's 13-year sentence, I asked if Christy and I could spend just a few minutes with Ryan since it had been over a year since we'd had any physical contact with Ryan. We had only visited him in jail where Ryan was behind glass. The judge denied us this request.

Ryan was sitting at a table, with his hands and legs shackled, just in front of Christy and me. As he stood up to leave, Ryan turned around and fell into Christy's arms for a gut-wrenching hug just before he was escorted out of the courtroom. I will never forget that moment as our son thrust his penitence into Christy's arms and begged her forgiveness. Heartbroken, Christy and I walked into the foyer with all the people who had come to support Ryan. Emotions were high and everyone was sobbing. I stood up on a chair and I addressed everyone who was there. Choking back my own grief, I thanked them all for coming and for their support. But, then I seized the moment to try to make something good come of this mess. I addressed the kids specifically. I told them, "You've just seen something happen here today to one of your really good friends that could easily happen to any of you if you pursue the same behavior. The next time anyone offers you a drink, or you're in a position to take drugs, smoke marijuana, or find yourself in a place where you need help, think about today. Think about Ryan, in his orange jumpsuit, hands and feet shackled, escorted by armed officers to a state penitentiary for the next 13 years. Think about that before you do anything that has to do with alcohol and drugs." It was a very dark day. But, there was also some closure. And, while the sentencing was a brutal reality check, the ordeal was finally over. I didn't need to spend any more energy on shortening Ryan's sentence. It was time to move on.

Very early on, when we visited Ryan in jail, we found a clear-headed, honest, respectful young man. As the weeks and months of jail time continued, the clarity in his speech, his ability to reason and his thought processes grew, and we became closer than we had been in years. I began to believe that my son's life was saved as a result of being caught and incarcerated. It was clear to me that Ryan's path prior to his arrest was so destructive, I couldn't stop it. Ryan had been a train wreck waiting to happen. In my heart's heart, I just didn't know when it would happen and, as a parent, that's a terrifying place to be. Christy and I were forced to turn him away from our home when we learned of his final drug relapse. We had no choice. But, part of me still whispered that, if only I could somehow keep him at home, I could keep him safe. In turning him away, I relinquished all my control and all of my ability to protect him. I knew that something bad would eventually happen.

It was always my goal as a father to provide solely for my family. Christy and I wanted to give our children the best opportunity to grow up in an environment that was loving, wholesome, and God-fearing. We wanted our boys' lives to be full of opportunities to be successful. I knew it was important that at least one of us be home with our kids, especially when they were little. So, it was my sacrifice to be the sole provider of finances and to do whatever it took—sometimes two or even three jobs, to make enough money to provide a good living and for Christy to stay home. We made the decision to move to a neighborhood that would put our kids into a safe, prosperous environment. I sacrificed a lot of time away from home when the boys were small, working sometimes as much as 65 to 70 hours a week. I didn't have a lot of opportunity to be involved with the boys until they were 4 and 6 years old, when I took a job that allowed me more time at home. However, whatever little time I did have, it was always spent at home. I loved to be with my family.

While my passion was baseball, I also shared Ryan's first love of football. He loved the San Francisco Forty-niners. I used to take both boys to watch the Niners' summer practice at Sierra College right in our hometown of Rocklin. Ryan and Justin would both hang on the chain link fence, watching their football heroes practice in the hot sun and then wait patiently to get autographs from greats like Jerry Rice or Joe Montana. I was able to coach Ryan in Junior Football and he was a tank. Ryan ran over people as a running back. He was big and strong and loved to play the game. I cherish the memories of that time with Ryan because it was before all the ugliness of the drugs began. We had real quality time out on that football field, with me encouraging Ryan to develop his talents and Ryan trying so hard to improve.

I have a great memory of Ryan as a little kid. I recall when he was about four years old and he had taken on an interesting persona. Christy, Ryan and I were all walking to the mail box. Ryan had on a black cape, a baseball cap, a Zorro mask, and a plastic pirate sword sticking out the back of his shorts. He was carrying an old army telephone and rambling on about how difficult life was. I looked at Christy and I said, "I think he's possessed." We laughed together, enjoying our son's personality, but noting that Ryan was a child of peaks and valleys. He was always really, really high or really, really low.

When Ryan was young, he always wanted me to lie down on the bed with him and tell him a story before he went to sleep. He loved it when I would make up stories, rather than just read one. I usually made up a story that evolved around an event of the day. We had some very fun birthday parties for Ryan. On Ryan's seventh birthday, Christy planned a pirate theme party. I hid "buried treasure" along the hillside of an undeveloped area of our neighborhood. I took all the neighbor kids to march off down the street with maps for the buried treasure. I still remember leading them in song to "A Pirate's Life for Me." Christy packed a lunch for us all and, as soon as the kids located all the buried treasure, they marched back to our house for cake and ice cream.

When Ryan began experimenting with drugs and alcohol I was completely unaware that he was exhibiting early warning signs of drug abuse. I perceived his angry outbursts, disobedience and disrespect to be simple adolescent defiance. I thought Ryan was just filled with hormones. I noted, however, that Ryan needed an enormous amount of sleep, which is a classic symptom of drug use. He would sleep for hours and hours until late into the afternoon. Ryan also started writing his own rap music lyrics, which Christy and I found. The language and the content of the lyrics included drugs and violence, and it was clear that Ryan was fascinated with the rap culture. I was unaware of the fact that such a fascination is another symptom of drug use. I should have paid more attention to Ryan's failing grades. Ryan was a very smart, intelligent kid and got excellent grades until middle school. In the eighth grade, he was suspended and midway through his freshman year, I saw him stalling out academically. I didn't see him progressing intellectually or vocationally.

Once Ryan entered drug counseling, he tried to maintain a normal lifestyle. He still loved football and went to the high school coach, confessing his problem with marijuana and asked for a chance to stay on the team. The coach graciously took the request to the team and collectively the team welcomed Ryan back. His teammates admired Ryan's courage and agreed to give him a second chance. There was a stipulation, however. According to school rules, Ryan was temporarily ineligible and would have to sit out six games. He could still be a team member and practice with the team, but he wouldn't be able to actually play in a game until late in the season. That consequence turned out to be more than Ryan could handle. For Ryan it was too long to wait and the pull of drugs became more important than not doing drugs and waiting six games to play.

This was a major turning point for Ryan, as he surrendered again to drugs. He quit football and Christy and I knew we needed to do something academically. Despite a grand gesture of intercession by another high school teacher, Ryan elected to leave high school and go on an independent study program. But, Ryan's success at that independent study lasted less than six weeks. The pull of drugs was far more demanding than schoolwork.

By this time, I'd set up a defense mechanism about Ryan. Our relationship had degraded to an all-time low. His verbal abuse had taken its toll. At that point, I just wanted him to get through some kind of education and be done. I was angry with Ryan while Christy's main reaction was worry for him. I did fear that something really bad could, and probably would, happen to him. I was also fed up with what we had to endure every day, not knowing where he was, who he was with and what drugs he was using. It was a living hell.

Christy and I tried to insulate Justin from a lot of what was happening with Ryan. Justin wasn't comfortable with deep conversations about something as serious as his brother being a drug addict. He kept busy with his school life, homework, friends, and sports and was consumed by his own world. I don't think Justin was fully aware of how serious things were with Ryan.

At the time of this writing, Ryan has served three of his 13-year sentence. Over the last two years I have watched him become a young man. He's grown up; he's an adult and he takes responsibility for his actions. He lives in a war zone and everywhere he turns there's an obstacle to overcome. Ryan's goals today are to simply get through each day, one day at a time. Looking forward, he has self-initiated his return to school, as the California correctional system does not offer any college training if you have more than five years on your sentence. He has enrolled in a California community college that accepts work through the U.S. Postal Service and I gladly pay for his tuition and books. Ryan does not have access to a computer, email or long distance learning through the internet. A snapshot of Ryan's life now includes a light on in his cell 24 hours a day. He shares a cell with another inmate. The cell consists of two bunks, a toilet and a sink. Ryan has to remove the mattress on his top bunk to sit up because the ceiling of the cell is not high enough to sit up on the bed. There is constant distraction, chatter, screaming, music, orders on the overhead paging system, and a million and one rules that must be followed to the letter. Ryan's always taken responsibility for his actions. He's never once blamed someone else for his crimes. He's made the statement multiple times that he deserves to be where he is. He is willing to pay society for his crimes.

Strange as it may sound, I couldn't be more proud of my son, Ryan, for the man that he has become. As a result of what he has gone through and where he is currently living, he is becoming molded and shaped into someone who is going to passionately contribute to our society once he's served his time. When I sit with him and talk with him now, it's a joy. He's so cognitively analytical. I think back to a time when Ryan could hardly remember his own name and I realize that today Ryan could easily thrive in any college in America. The tragedy that our family has suffered, the events that have led us to this place today, have redefined our outlook on life. Christy and I know how painful it can be to lose a son. No, our son's not dead, but he was taken from us. Ryan has been extracted from our family and we can no longer enjoy his company as we knew it before he was incarcerated. I never ever want anyone to go through what Christy and I have gone through with Ryan.

TEN

FROM JUSTIN: I'VE FORGIVEN MY BROTHER

I always looked up to my brother. But, even when we were little kids, Ryan was extremely competitive. He always had to win at everything. He'd even cheat to win. Ryan was bigger and stronger than me, although occasionally I'd beat him at basketball or video games and that was hard for him. He never wanted his little brother to beat him at anything. Growing up, he was always trying to "toughen me up." Ryan would punch me in the arm and I was so skinny, it would usually hurt.

Ryan and I used to play video games. I loved to play Nintendo® Mega Man because together we could beat the game. We played Contra, which required two people to play. We built forts between our rooms with blankets, sheets, rope and all the snacks we could sneak out of the kitchen.

When I was in seventh grade, our family went on a cruise to Ensenada, Mexico, San Diego and Catalina Island. I had the best time hanging out with Ryan. We went shopping together in Mexico and he'd help me bargain with the merchants for better prices. When Ryan first started using drugs, he became nicer to me. I didn't know Ryan was on drugs, but I did notice he was different. Ryan was less competitive and less intense. Willingly, he'd let me hang out with him and his friends. One thing I'll give Ryan credit for is that he never offered me drugs and he wouldn't let his friends include me in their drug world. I remember once when Ryan's friends were all ready to go out back and smoke (probably marijuana), and his friends invited me to come with them. Ryan spoke up and said, "No, he's not coming with us." When I found out Ryan was using drugs, I didn't tell anyone. It was sort of hard to figure out. But I wasn't going to "tell" on my brother. It was all sort of a new concept to me. Doing drugs wasn't really on my list of things to do.

I wish I'd known...*(Christy writes) There is a teenage code of ethics. It's a fact that teenagers, will not "rat out" their friends. Even when teens are worried about their friends, even when they know friends are in danger and on a destructive path, teenagers will not violate the unspoken code of loyalty. Teens don't tell. Don't expect to get information from siblings or friends of your child if you think drugs or alcohol might be a problem.*

Sadness is not the first emotion I experienced when Ryan was arrested. I was angry. I couldn't believe that my brother would do something like that. I had never seen my mom cry before and I hated the sight of it. Seeing my mom so devastated is the worst thing I had ever experienced. There was nothing I could do to make her feel better. I wanted more than anything to be able to see my brother—not to hug him, but to hit him for the pain he had caused my family. He had put our family through so much and the drugs, failed treatments, crimes and the arrest were terrible for Mom, Dad and me. But, I've forgiven Ryan. He's my brother and I love him. I see him every few weeks and he's become an honorable person. He sent me a card recently, apologizing for not being a good role model for me during my teenage years and for not being able to attend my high school graduation. I think it was hard for him to write those words. I'm over it. But, I'm not sure Ryan will ever be over it.

When I see Ryan now, I see the guy who was always fun to be with. He's happy now. He's the same person he was before the drugs, but nicer. I visit him when I can, but I don't think he really knows me that well. When he's released from prison, I want to rekindle a relationship with him and for him to be a regular part of my life. I am not interested in using drugs or alcohol, although there's plenty of opportunity. I used to go to parties and I chose to not participate in the alcohol or drugs. But now, I've just decided not to even go to parties anymore. It's boring. I have so many things to look forward to. I'm going to the University of California at Davis, where I'll play college baseball and pursue my dreams. I'd like to play professional baseball one day and I want a career in the medical field. I want to become a physician or a physician's assistant. Drugs and alcohol do not fit in any of these plans.

ELEVEN

FROM COUNSELORS, COMMUNITY AND FRIENDS:
LESSONS FROM RYAN'S STORY

F*rom Counselor Michael Moncrieff,*
     (Ryan's drug and alcohol counselor)

Drugs serve many purposes. From a cultural perspective, drug and alcohol use are an inherent part of American life. For a kid growing up in just about any neighborhood in this country, he or she will be exposed to this piece of American life. This history of drug and alcohol use is so entrenched in our culture that, despite laws aimed at prohibiting or controlling their use, they will always be present. It is arguably unavoidable. Unfortunately, America's drug and alcohol use are a shadow of the enlightened image we strive for in this country.

One might look at drugs and alcohol from the perspective of a family's values. Many kids grow up in families that have permissive values about drug and alcohol use. Parents may use drugs and alcohol themselves and, though they may discourage its use, they essentially teach their children a way of life. As a counselor, many times I heard a parent share that they felt okay about their kids doing tempered alcohol or marijuana use. They would often cite their own successful use of pot and alcohol as evidence of its harmlessness. This was, of course, until their child's use of pot and alcohol suddenly stopped being harmless or until they learned that their child's use had progressed into the use of other less "acceptable" drugs. In my opinion, although addiction has multiple causes, it is most rooted in the family.

Another perspective, which may explain the role of drug use in our society, is that some children seek alcohol and drug use as a formidable rite of passage. There may be a basic human instinct to seek difficult life experiences in order to grow and develop. If the family or our American culture does not offer a child real and formidable challenges to force the development of character and strengths, they may seek it on their own. In older cultures, and in many foreign cultures, rituals exist to challenge and develop children as they come of age. Many of our children do this via addiction. The problem, of course, is that addiction as a rite of passage fails to create positive results. Sobriety and recovery can complete this developmental process for some adolescents, enabling them to progress successfully into young adulthood. There is much more that can be said about the role of drugs in our society, but I think those are a few important thoughts about what awaits our children as they age in their world.

I have many thoughts about Ryan's case and the experience did affect me tremendously. I flash back on the last conversations we had before he was arrested. He was in full-blown relapse and getting worse by the day. Christy had contacted me for advice and she was scared for his safety and the harm that might come to the family. I know how hurt she and Rick were as parents and how deeply they wanted Ryan to understand the love they had for him. I remember Christy's worry about Ryan's influence on his younger brother. We talked about intervention. We talked about being ready when he showed up again, looking for the rescue. We all knew it would come at some point. I advised Christy to be ready to offer him help—something that he could access immediately. I advised her to express love to him, but to only offer him help.

Ryan finally did show up and Christy and Rick did everything I suggested. Ryan's response was that he needed to think about it. Over the next week or so, Ryan would make the greatest mistakes of his life. I have wondered about my advice to Christy and Rick. I've thought that maybe if I had told them to just get him home and offer him help later, then none of this would have happened. But, from all of my experience with Ryan, I knew that Ryan wouldn't go easily and I thought he needed to be forced into receiving help. I wonder if as a counselor I should have held him more accountable. When Ryan was clean and sober, he was the most fantastic human being. On several occasions, he stayed late after group talking with me and playing with my daughter. I saw this miraculous shift in him and maybe I was too happy for this great kid. I wanted that for him and maybe I got too nice.

When Ryan was struggling, I cared so much for him that I tolerated some of his unacceptable attitudes and behaviors just so that he would keep coming to me for counsel. Maybe if I had been more assertive and direct with him, things would've turned out differently. But again, I gave Ryan as much as I had to give at the time. I taught him everything I could teach him. I challenged him in ways that hurt both him and me. I undermined his disease of addiction in every way I could think, especially by continuing to speak with both of his parents to try to stop his self-destruction. Personally, this experience devastated me. I weep for Ryan and I weep for Ryan's family. Because my personal sobriety started in such a similar way with a similarly loving family, I've always felt connected to Ryan. As he did well, I cheered inside and as he struggled, I, too, struggled inside with what to do. I have watched clients die. I have watched friends in sobriety die. Ryan's experience was right on the same level, with the one saving grace that he remains alive and has the opportunity to live a different life.

Just as Rick, Christy and Justin have taken this tragedy and attempted to create miracles for others, I too have tried to do the same. Ryan's story became a regular part of teaching the kids about the horrible realities of this disease. Ryan's story teaches of the delicate security that we all have, that the smallest mistakes can lead to huge consequences. The Crandells' efforts as a family teach that even the most painful life experiences can be transformed into useful wisdom to help others. As those before me gave so freely to help me, I have tried to do the same for those in my work … in my life.

It is so important for parents to be vigilant and informed because it may save their child's life. First, children can be real addicts. As well, children can suffer real mental illness, which can be equally as devastating as it is for adults. One can even argue that addiction and mental illness for children are more damaging because children lack the internal skills to deal with these problems. Also, there is a bad chemistry that happens with teenagers and drug use, where they use drugs and alcohol in a particularly aggressive and destructive manner. Teens use differently and, as such, their use is particularly dangerous. It's not the same as adults. The purpose of the drug or the beer or the party IS to get wasted. If addiction runs in your family, heed the hereditary risk. Most addicts in recovery will tell you that with all things equal in life, the one difference between them and anyone else is that when the drug is ingested, there is an overwhelming experience of desire for more.

This strange reaction to the drug is what makes an addict an addict. And it's nobody's fault that this exists. It just does. It is the one difference that every addict wants to believe they don't have because, if it's not true, then they actually will be able to control their drug and alcohol use. It is my belief that this will be the thing that research identifies as the difference. This "phenomenon of craving" will be the genetic difference that gets discovered. If your child appears to have this obsessive/compulsive quality in their drug or alcohol use (and one can tell because there begins to develop a genuine love relationship with the substance), then it is very likely, despite their age or socioeconomic background, that they have the disease of addiction. It is so important for parents to be vigilant and informed because they have the ability to prevent drug use and its associated problems. If drug use and its problems have already surfaced, then the sooner and more effectively they intervene, the more likely that their children will be helped.

There is a powerful statistic that states the sooner that a child uses drugs and alcohol the more likely that they will develop a legitimate and diagnosable problem. It is my belief that a similar thing can happen with helping children. The sooner they are helped, then the more likely that they will get well. These behaviors exist in patterns over time and changing these behaviors will also require changing the patterns over time. As we often hear, recovery is a process. The sooner a parent acts assertively and powerfully, not weakly and fearfully, the sooner these problems will improve.

From Attorney Tom Leupp,
(Ryan's defense attorney)

Ryan's case was an especially powerful and tragic example of how drugs can transform a person and nearly destroy him. I have seen many cases of drug devastation, usually methamphetamine. It is a powerful and insidious drug that can really take over a person and essentially make them into someone else. Recently, I have seen some cases where Oxycontin had the same effect.

Ryan's case was unusual in my practice due to his sudden string of violent felony conduct, although, as you are aware, violent and aggressive conduct is common in people with drug addiction. Ryan's case was a sad example of why mandatory sentencing laws are frequently simply too harsh. The ten-year enhancement for gun use provided no deterrence. Because of his mental state, a thousand year enhancement would have had no deterrent effect. If deterrence were truly a goal, then these laws would be well-publicized and presented in high school. The goal is not deterrence, but brutal punishment. Ryan was actually facing 65 years due to mandatory sentencing laws, and it took a great deal of effort and a responsible and decent prosecutor to get his sentence down to 13 years. A justice system that exacts that sort of mandatory punishment when a person with a serious drug problem has no significant record, a fine family and other support systems, is seriously flawed. I know that the system is seriously flawed and I do not expect that we will soon see our country move toward more compassionate or even rational punishment.

I will continue to do whatever I can for each client faced with such punishment because I know that they are individuals who must have their "side of the story" presented. It was a privilege, however painful and poignant, to represent Ryan and his fine family. I am heartened to know that Ryan is doing well in difficult circumstances, and I am confident that he will emerge someday as a good and strong man with a bright future. I will be here to embrace him and assist him, and it will be a pleasure to do so.

From Karen Meusling,
(Supervising United States Probation Officer, Sacramento, CA)

Drug addiction can happen to anyone. In my experience, the difference isn't the socioeconomic background, it's the types of drugs that are abused, which are often based on the selling price of a particular drug. The far-reaching impact drugs have on our society are too numerous to count. The individual consequences include, but are not limited to: loss of job and income; failure in school; loss of family and friends; homelessness; committing crimes to obtain money for drugs (i.e. ending up in prison); and self-esteem.

In the federal system, in the year 2005, 34.2% of all defendants sentenced were for drug crimes. This is the greatest percentage for the types of crimes which come into the federal system. The crimes we have seen more frequently in the last couple of years related to drug use are identity theft crimes. By obtaining the identification of another person, either by mail theft or bank fraud, a person is able to obtain money illegally to buy drugs. It is said that drug addiction is a disease and this is true. The likelihood of a "rehabilitated" drug user, returning to the use of drugs, is alarmingly high in my line of work. It is a daily struggle for those who have been or are addicted and it is only with the help, love and support of family, friends and professionals that the addict can hope to overcome addiction and return to a law-abiding, productive lifestyle.

From Danny,
(Ryan's cousin, age 7 at the time of Ryan's arrest)

I was in the kitchen when my mom told me Ryan had been arrested. She said that Ryan went into a gas station with a gun and he's now in jail for 13 years. I was scared and I was sad. Mostly I was shocked. Ryan was one of my favorite people in my life. We went swimming together a lot and hung out just to talk together. Ryan cared about me and he told me 24/7 that I was his best buddy. He was my hero before he was arrested. But, after he started using drugs and got arrested, I kind of thought he was a traitor. I didn't want him to be away from me for 13 years and it was his fault that he would be locked up in jail for so long. It was all because of him doing marijuana and all those drugs that now I couldn't see him.

When I heard he was reading the Bible in jail and he was trying to get more into God, I felt better about Ryan. I felt better that he was more like my old buddy. I forgave him. I'll be 21 years old when Ryan is released from prison. I want Ryan to be a part of my life when he's released. Because of Ryan's experience with drugs and alcohol, I'm never going to do drugs. I'm going to watch out for it very much. I know that's a horrible life. I've heard it from Ryan. I talk to Ryan on the phone. It doesn't matter that he's in prison. I want Ryan to be in my life now and after he's out of jail. He's still my hero.

***

From Kaitlin,
(Ryan's neighborhood friend)

Growing up, there never seemed to be anything that could stand in my way. Ryan was always my "big brother." We would fight like brother and sister, get put in time-out like brother and sister and love like a brother and sister. When Ryan was arrested, it felt like my world stopped. It felt like nothing in the universe would ever be the same. The equilibrium of the entire planet was thrown off. I felt like this utter state of confusion, shock, disappointment and shame would never go away. Kids at school had something witty and humorous to say, some parents whispered and gawked, society gossiped and twisted the stories, and embarrassment struck close family and friends. I wondered, how could this turmoil and chaos surrounding our streets ever be forgotten or forgiven.

***

From Erin,
(A mom in our neighborhood)

"Happy Milburn Street," that's what the kids liked to call it. A group of families moved into this brand-new community on the same weekend and began to raise our kids. Ryan was the oldest of what would be 18 children, most of them born on this small street in Rocklin. From the first, this was everything we always wanted. Family barbecues, kids playing in the front yard, street hockey, flashlight tag, camping trips—the perfect childhood. We lived next door to the Crandells for 14 years. They were like family to us. We parented each others' children and had free access to each others' homes. Half the time we didn't lock the doors, or even close the garage doors at night. We shared tools, projects, parties, personal crises and celebrations.

Ryan was always the leader of the pack. All the kids followed his lead. He came up with the games and mostly made the rules, usually to his advantage. My youngest daughter followed him around one entire summer and adoringly called him, "my superman." He was a boy with a great smile, a warm heart, a brain for math and a wild streak. As he grew up, there would be signs that he was looking for trouble or trouble was looking for him. When I learned of Ryan's arrest, I think the first thing to register was absolute shock. Afterwards, I remember being very angry—angry at Ryan for the pain he caused his family whom I love. Angry at the loss of innocence he inflicted on all the children, mine included. Angry at him for the many blessings he squandered with the path he chose. But, there was also a huge sense of loss and heartbreak because I loved him, too. As a group, we talked about little else for a long time, trying to make sense of what happened and how each of us might have contributed. What could we have done differently in our encounters with Ryan to change this tragic outcome?

I was asked to speak as a character witness at the sentencing hearing. I had a huge range of conflicting emotions: I wanted to help, I loved this boy, but I also believed in my gut that crimes using weapons for threat and intimidation should be severely punished. I didn't want that kind of crime in my community, threatening my safety and the safety of my kids. I felt really torn between pleading for this boy to be returned to his family to give them another opportunity to turn him around and what I thought would be a just punishment for a crime if committed by anyone else. On the witness stand I remember him smiling at me, that smile lit up his face like the innocent child he was when I met him, and my heart just broke. That hearing was so much like death. I felt us all eulogizing a living boy who was present for the occasion. There were so many tears. This event changed us all forever.

Everyone who loves the Crandell family was altered by this 24-hour period in Ryan's life. Our community was tainted and is not so idyllic anymore. But, our eyes were opened and other kids have been saved as a result. Sometimes reality smacks you hard—like a two-by-four over the head. This definitely got our attention.

From Ashly,
(Ryan's friend at school)

It had been months since I last talked to Ryan when I heard from a family friend that he had been arrested. Ryan and I became friends during our freshman year of high school in our Language Arts class, where he and I cracked jokes about the characters we outlined in our dialectical journals. I enjoyed his sense of humor, crazy jokes and love of music, which he sung under his breath whenever he wasn't laughing. That summer Ryan and I stopped talking. I had heard he was into drinking and some drugs. He didn't initiate contact and I didn't either, rationalizing this by thinking that we were probably just classroom acquaintances rather than actual friends. This made me sad because what attracted me to Ryan were the core values he expressed in his sensitivity to my feelings, his sentimental affection for his girlfriend and his sincerity towards his friends.

Ryan is a natural leader in my opinion, and it brought surprise, deep sadness, fear and lost hope when he was arrested and then sentenced. After the sentencing, my first thought was, "How can I talk to him now?" Ryan and I began to exchange letters and right away I admired his determination to avoid further drug use. He is now dedicated to his family and friends. His letters became my inspiration and strength and, to this day, Ryan is an example to me. After visiting him, my face is sore from smiling and laughing the whole time. Ryan reminds me to take one day at a time, pray and stick to my values. I count Ryan as one of my true friends.

From Susan,
(Ryan's aunt)

When I first found out that Ryan had committed armed robbery, I had such mixed feelings. I was with my sister, Christy, when she was told of Ryan's arrest. The desperation I saw in her face was horrendous! To witness the utter pain, turmoil and shattering of a parent at such a time, left me feeling completely helpless and heartbroken. My first feelings were of helplessness, then anger that Ryan could do this to his parents who had given him such a great life with all the possibilities of success. Then, in a matter of minutes, my feelings turned toward Ryan. This poor young boy was left all alone with a hard reality ahead of him.

Ryan was always such a caring, loving, observant young boy, yet this boy we hardly knew anymore. I thought about my own kids and wondered what I was going to tell them and how this was going to impact them. Our families are very close and we often had family dinners and celebrated every holiday together. My children would definitely notice their cousin missing. How was I supposed to break this type of news to such innocent little ones who had no idea of what I was going to tell them? I was frustrated at this reality. I thought I would give myself a little time to prepare what I would say, but that was shattered as soon as my second grader came home from school, wondering if we owned a gas station because his cousin had robbed one with a gun. This is how my sweet little 7-year-old was told about his cousin. He guessed it was Ryan without anyone telling him because our family had been praying for Ryan over the past year or so.

When we found out the extent of Ryan's sentence, it seemed surreal. How could my little nephew with the big heart, the one who always noticed anything different about a person, who was always so polite and caring of others, be facing a 13 year sentence? This was a boy whose mother was the stay-at-home mom on top of it all, whose father coached his baseball teams, the boy whose friends always migrated to his house with a parent always home; how could this have happened to him? Then I got freaked out, thinking that if it can happen to my sister's family then it can happen to mine! I had three small children (ages 7, 5 and 2) and I thought that by being involved in everything and giving them a good foundation I could prevent this type of thing from happening to them. I believed that I could keep them away from drugs because I thought that the children with drug problems were the ones who had no supervision and had problems at home. I couldn't have been more mistaken and at this time that cold hard reality hit me! I came to realize my children's lives are their own and they will make their own choices along their life paths. This is a scary thought and it gives me no comfort. There will be nothing I can do if my children decide to make poor choices and to meddle in drugs and alcohol, except for one thing—educate myself about drug abuse and be aware of the signs and seek help.

Our whole family looks forward to each visit we have with Ryan. I love the little things he tells my children about making good choices and doing the right thing. He has a way of informing them without too much detail, but gets the point through. My children look up to Ryan. As a result of Ryan's ordeal, I look at others in a different way and am much less judgmental. Ryan reminds me that there are a lot of good people in prison, people with good hearts and I don't think I would have ever thought that before. He's helped me realize that drug abuse is a choice, but drug addiction is a disease and that it is darned near impossible for one to stop without professional help. Who would have thought that my young drug-addicted nephew, who has completely turned his life around, could teach his aunt such lessons?

From Dana,
(Our neighbor)

I will never forget that Sunday afternoon when Christy called to say that Ryan had been arrested. I was shopping with my daughters. I shakily walked outside and sat on the curb to hear the few details she shared and her request for prayer. After we hung up, I was dazed and numb. It was the oddest thing to finish my errands while subconsciously rolling around the fact in my head that Christy's world had been shattered. We spent that next day together. I picked up Christy and brought her to my house. We talked and I fed her. I wanted so badly to make her okay! I was so mad at Ryan! How could he do this to his mother? And yet, I have always had a soft spot for Ryan in my heart and, when I considered how he must have been feeling at that time, my anger would dissolve and turn to a deep sadness. What would become of him? How was he doing, really doing, incarcerated? How could drugs take such a hold of someone, to turn this fun-loving, friendly, soft-hearted, yet intense kid into a criminal? I was so worried about Christy—how would she ever be able to pick up the pieces and go on? I was worried about Justin and the pressure he must have felt and must still feel to be "the good one." I was selfishly angry that Ryan had changed my most cheerful and attentive friend forever!

I was hesitant to tell my own children and compromise their innocence (they were 14, 11 and 9), and especially to tell Keith, my youngest, who idolized Ryan. I became afraid of what might someday happen with my kids because Christy was the perfect mom! She stayed home with her kids their entire childhood, she always had fun and creative things to do with them, she was the cool mom on the block. If it could happen to her kid, it could happen to anyone's kid! The misuse and abuse of drugs suddenly became a reality, not something that I read about in the paper or heard about in second person. Our sweet little neighborhood community was forever changed by the entrance of drugs into Ryan's life. Even though I try to rely on God for peace and comfort, I am much more afraid of the social pressures and choices available to our teens.

There has also been a positive affect brought about by Ryan's incarceration. Certainly, we've shared more dialogue about drug use, both with Christy and my other friends, and with my children. The introduction and impact of RCASA (what a wonderful program) and Christy's faith and testimony, have touched many lives. Most importantly, Ryan's maturity and freedom from drug addiction have led him to become a wonderful young man.

From Julie,
(A close family friend)

We were in Mendocino when we got the phone call. We had seen Ryan on the news. We were shocked and immediately drove home to be with the Crandell family. Rick and Christy had tried so hard to help him. At least now they knew where he was. Telling our children was very hard. Our son looked up to Ryan, our oldest daughter and Ryan had been very close and our middle daughter was already showing signs of shutting down. We had lost many loved ones in the years prior to this – how could we tell them about losing Ryan, too? For days, there was only sadness and waiting. Our kids felt that everyone they loved kept going away. There was nothing we could do except pray and try to help Rick, Christy and Justin through what would be the most difficult time in their lives.

Rumors flew around the school and my son came home angry, knowing Ryan had put him in an uncomfortable situation. He wanted to protect Ryan and set straight any discrepancies or rumors, but it just hurt him more. It was at this time that my son started going downhill himself. I went with Christy to visit Ryan in Placer County Jail. I was nervous and didn't know how I was going to handle it or what I was going to say to him. When he came in he was in an orange jumpsuit, looking very pale. He placed his hand on the glass between us and that's when I knew our lives would never be the same.

My youngest son entered junior high with a heavy heart and a huge chip on his shoulder. He started hanging out with the wrong people, his grades started slipping and eventually he turned to drugs. Our son started acting just like Ryan had and it scared us to death. Ironically, he ended up in the same rehabilitation facility Ryan went to and is now doing much better. From prison, Ryan counseled with our son several times about how drugs can ruin your life. They have a close relationship now. I don't think a day goes by that I don't think about Ryan. He is so humble and it makes me love him so much more. I see a man now where there was a boy. When I hug him, I don't want to let go. I think how easy it is for me to walk out those prison gates and how sad that makes me. But if Ryan can endure it, so can I. I think Ryan will change the lives of many along his journey. I pray for God to keep him safe and out of harm's way.

From Lori,
(Ryan's grandmother)

In the months leading up to Ryan's arrest, I felt like I was holding my breath. Seeing him at family gatherings or staying at his house when his folks were away, I always felt he was trying too hard to act and feel normal. I could see in his eyes the struggle to be liked against the drive to be cool. The day we came home to find out about his arrest and crimes, I just went numb. I worried about my daughter having a breakdown as she collapsed at the news. As time passed, I wondered how this could happen to our family because, as an acquaintance put it, "your family seems to be under a lucky star!" It still hits me at odd times that this tragedy really happened and that Ryan will be in prison for so long. When we visit Ryan I am struck by how composed and mature he has become and I pray that somehow his sentence will be shortened. I am saddened by the toll this has taken on his mother and father, each doing what they can to make something good come from this.

From John,
(Ryan's grandfather)

I always saw that Ryan was a hard-headed kid – very hard to penetrate his shell. It just seemed to me he wouldn't cooperate with anyone or anything. He needed to have a vision or a goal and he had neither one. We were at one another's throat most of the time. I didn't please him and he didn't please me. We got to the point where we barely talked to one another. Upon the actual arrest, I was very disappointed in Ryan and his lack of judgment, but that was typical of him in the way he was going. I was more disappointed for my daughter, Christy, and son-in-law, Rick, for what he put them through. I was very disappointed in the sentencing he received, but I have to respect the law and its penalties.

As I look back on the situation I feel that it was probably one of the best things that could have happened to Ryan. I have visited him several times in prison and I can see he is a changed man. It's just too bad his sentence had to be so long because I believe if Ryan were out of prison now, he'd be an asset to society.

From Roc,
(Ryan's former high school teacher)

For me personally, I've gone through several different stages since Ryan's arrest. It wasn't just one feeling, but a myriad of feelings and then the progression of becoming aware of the gravity of the situation. At first, I was in pain for Ryan and when I went to visit him in jail it was shock to me. I then felt really bad for Rick and Christy. It has been difficult to watch how it has affected them. As time went on, however, I realized it was a necessary thing for Ryan. For kids in the community, I think things are "out of sight, out of mind." They get caught up in the drama of the moment but eventually are going to do what they are going to do when they're in the moment. What happened to Ryan is not really affecting them now. I don't think they can remember that far back. I wish they could.

I think Rick and Christy have made something positive out of the tragedy with the RCASA group and bringing Parent Project® to Rocklin. Initially, after Ryan's arrest a lot of parents were very concerned about drugs and it had a huge initial impact. But now, most people have gone back to their regular lives and moved on. Some people think about it on a regular basis and know it was something that could happen to anybody at anytime and they guard against it, but I don't think everybody does.

From Erik,
(Ryan's best friend)

Ryan had always been my best friend. We grew up together, living across the street from each other. He was the kind of guy that would do anything for you no matter what the consequences. With Ryan there was never a dull moment. He always had something to do and he always had tons of friends to do it with. I thought that Ryan could do whatever he wanted when he was older because he was so good at talking. He could seemingly talk his way out of any situation, never missing a beat. I looked up to him, amazed at how he could make friends with anyone in any situation.

Ryan and I did everything together, but the first time he smoked weed, I wasn't with him. I felt like I was always the conscience on his shoulder, telling him what to and not to do. If I told Ryan to go and do something funny, he would do it willingly, just to get me to laugh. However, if he had something that he wanted to do that might get him or both of us in a lot of trouble, I would try to talk him out of it. Don't get me wrong, we had our share of trouble-making, but it was limited to sneaking out at night and pointing lasers at people in stores when we were younger. We never did anything that would get us in trouble with the law, but it was always stuff our parents wouldn't particularly like. So, I believe that Ryan began to smoke without telling me because he knew what I would say.

Going to different high schools had a huge impact on our friendship. Before high school we were constantly at each others' houses, spending the night whenever we got the chance. So, when I look back, I feel that if I had just gone to his school, maybe all of this wouldn't have happened. Maybe I could have been there to kind of talk him out of it. But I wasn't. I went to the school that really focused on college. I was in a sort of bubble where my friends and classmates all seemed to care a lot about the future. This is when I think it began to put a strain on our relationship. Ryan and I used to always be together, but now we went to different schools and Ryan had more time to hang out with different people. Ryan used to tell me everything, but after he started to smoke and use other drugs, he wasn't as honest. I remember when I would ask him what he did on a particular Friday night, he would tell me part of the story, but never the whole story. It was only later that I would learn the full extent of his story.

By the end of my junior year, I barely saw Ryan. Once Ryan's drug use was exposed, I didn't hang out with him much. This forced Ryan to hang out with other people more often. I wasn't there to be that conscience on his shoulder, giving him advice about what he should do. For me, I saw that a lot of teens and especially my friends were doing drugs, so I didn't really see a huge problem with it. I first saw that his drug use was a problem when Ryan told me that he was stealing over-the-counter medication from grocery stores. He told me that he and a friend had gone to every store in Rocklin and that there wasn't a single box of Coricidan left. I was still in denial. I always thought that he would get past this if he was just able to learn on his own, because I knew that Ryan always had to learn things the hard way.

I first found out about the robberies on the evening news. I couldn't believe it. I still didn't know the extent of the problem until I talked to Rick and Christy and found out what Ryan was facing. After I found out the entire story about his robbery spree, I couldn't help but wonder what would have happened if I could have prevented this. But after a while, I started to think that maybe this was good for Ryan. Toward the end, he seemed to be on a downward spiral. At least now I know that he can have a future and that he's alive and safe. I'm still very proud of Ryan. I think that, given the circumstances, he is handling his sentence very well, making the best of his situation and not dwelling on the past.

TWELVE

Resources for Parents, Drug Charts & FAQ's

SYMPTOMS AND SIGNS OF DRUG USE

Normal adolescent angst can resemble symptoms of drug use. Parents bringing their child to a treatment center often report that they see no symptoms of substance abuse.

- Loss of motivation, apathy
- Change in sleeping patterns, sleeping too much or too little
- Withdrawal from family and regular activities
- Changes in friends
- Lying
- Secretiveness on the phone or computer
- Drop in grades
- Truancy, skipping classes
- Discipline problems at school
- Disinterest in personal grooming
- Change in appetite or weight
- Cough, stuffy nose or frequent sniffling
- Dilated or constricted pupils or bloodshot eyes
- Tobacco smell on clothes
- Over-reaction to mild criticism, rage, emotional outbursts, moodiness, depression, anxiety, irritability, over-sensitivity, hostility
- Disappearance of money or items of value at home
- Drugs, drug paraphernalia, eye drops

Type of Drug	Street Names
Amphetamine	Biphetamine, Dexedrine; Black Beauties, Crosses, Hearts, Speed, Uppers
Cocaine	Coke, Crack, Flake, Rocks, Snow, Blow
Methamphetamines	Desoxyn; Crank, Crystal, Glass, Ice, Speed
Nicotine	Cigars, Cigarettes, Smokeless Tobacco, Snuff, Spit Tobacco
Phencyclidines	PCP; Angel Dust, Boat, Hog, Love Boat, Ozone, Wack, Rocket fuel
Ecstasy/MDMA	XTC, X, Adam, Clarity, Lover's Speed, Fizz

Physical Signs and Symptoms	Method of Use	Drug Detection Times
Increased energy, irritability, anxious, restless, loss of appetite	Injected, oral, smoked, sniffed	1-4 days
Impaired thinking, confused, anxious, depressed, short tempered, panic attacks, suspiciousness, dilated pupils, sleeplessness, loss of appetite, decreased sexual drive, restlessness, irritability, very talkative, scratching, hallucinations, paranoia	Injected, smoked, sniffed	1-4 days
"Wired," sleeplessness for days and weeks at a time, total loss of appetite, extreme weight loss, dialated pupils, excited, talkative, deluded sense of power, paranoia, depression, loss of control, nervousness, unusual sweating, shaking, anxiety, hallucinations, aggression, violence, dizziness, mood changes, blurred vision, mental confusion, agitation	Injected, oral, smoked, sniffed	3-5 days
Addictive. Increased risk of lung cancer and cardiovascular disease	Smoked, sniffed, oral, transdermal	1-3 days for light smoking, can be detected up to 2 weeks for heavy smoking
Shallow breathing, flushing, profuse sweating, loss of balance, dizziness, blurred vision, nausea, vomiting, hallucinations, paranoia	Injected, oral, smoked	2-8 days
Dehydration, euphoria, hallucinations, involuntary teeth clenching/grinding, muscle cramps, reduced inhibitions, dilated pupils, heightened sense of alertness	Oral	1-2 days

Type of Drug	Street Names
Marijuana	Blunt, Grass, Herb, Pot, Reefer, Weed, Ganga, Aunt Mary, Skunk, Boom, Gansta, Kif
Oxycontin, Darvon, Vicodin, Dilaudid, Demerol	Oxy, OC
Heroin	Diacetylmorphine; Horse, Smack
Alcohol	Beer, Wine, Liquor
Barbiturates	Amytal, Nembutal, Secondal, Phenobarbital; Barbs
Benzodiazepines	Ativan, Halcion, Librium, Rohypnol, Valium; Roofies, Tranks, Xanax, T-bars
Inhalants	Huffing, Bagging

Physical Signs and Symptoms	Method of Use	Drug Detection Times
Compulsive eating, bloodshot red eyes that are squinty (they may have trouble keeping them open), dry mouth, excessive and uncontrollable laughter, forgetfulness, short term memory loss, extreme lethargy, delayed motor skills, occasional paranoia, hallucinations, laziness, lack of motivation, stupidity, sickly sweet smell on body, hair, and clothes, and strong mood changes and behaviors when the person is "high"	Oral, smoked	1 day - 6 weeks, depending on frequency of use and body mass
Drowsiness, general sense of well being, euphoria vomiting, loss of appetite, sweating, impaired vision	Oral, crushed and snorted	1-3 days
Chemically enforced euphoria. "Nodding," which is a dreamlike state, near sleep, drifting off for minutes or hours. For long time abusers heroin may act like a stimulant and they can do a normal daily routine; however, for others, it leaves them completely powerless to do anything	Injected, smoked, sniffed	1-3 days
Decreased inhibition, slowed motor coordination, lethargy, relaxed muscles, staggering gait, poor judgment, slow, uncertain reflexes, disorientation, and slurred speech	Oral	6-10 hours
Decreased inhibition, slowed motor coordination, lethargy, relaxed muscles, staggering gait, poor judgment, slow, uncertain reflexes, disorientation, and slurred speech	Injected, oral	2-10 days
Decreased inhibition, slowed motor coordination, lethargy, relaxed muscles, staggering gait, poor judgment, slow, uncertain reflexes, disorientation, and slurred speech	Injected, oral	3-7 days
Short-lasting euphoria, giggling, silliness, dizziness, loss of coordination, loss of appetite, nausea, sneezing, coughing, nosebleeds, fatigue, disorientation, unconsciousness	Inhaled through the mouth and nose	

NO-NONSENSE ACTION PLAN

What to do if you find evidence of drugs or alcohol:

1. Stay calm and develop a game plan so that you will be prepared for action when you confront your teen.

2. Call your health insurance company and research where you can take your teen for an assessment. Make an appointment.

3. Confront your teen at the earliest opportunity and be ready to impose consequences, if necessary, to get your teen to the assessment appointment.

4. Remind your teen you love him or her and will do whatever it takes to keep him or her safe.

FREQUENTLY ASKED QUESTIONS

1. I don't want to lose my son's trust by drug-testing him. Is there another way to find out if he's using drugs?

Yes, you can catch him red-handed, but by waiting until that happens, you have let precious time go by. Explain to your teen that you love him so much, you're willing to do whatever it takes to keep him safe. That includes random drug testing.

Early intervention is the best chance for successful intervention. Try to think of drug testing as a way for your child to EARN your trust and to prove he is trustworthy. Unfortunately, kids are so good at covering up their drug use that, by the time you catch him, it may be that he is well down the road to abuse.

Remember, statistics show that by the time a child is caught using drugs or alcohol, the average time that child has been using is 7-8 months. Don't wait. And, remember that drug testing gives your teen an excellent excuse to "say no to drugs" that is accepted by his peers.

2. Where can I find drug test kits?

We are fortunate here in Rocklin in that our Police Department provides them at cost to the public. Check with your local law enforcement to find out if drug testing kits are available.

One of the best websites to purchase drug test kits is at www.drugtestyourteen.com. This site also has some good information about drug testing. You can find drug tests at your local store pharmacy, however they are often much more expensive.

3. I suspect my child is using drugs, but his drug tests are coming up negative. What should I do?

First of all, remember to listen to that "gut-check" that tells you something is not right. Here are a few suggestions:

- Make sure you are randomly testing.

- If possible, make sure the test is being observed by a same-sex parent or trusted friend or relative. Kids have been known to substitute another person's clean urine.

- Take a urine sample on a Friday night, but don't test the sample, just throw it away. Some teens think that after they've been tested, it is a license to party for the next few days. Surprise him with another test on Sunday morning. If this still comes up negative, try searching his room or car when he's not around and look for signs of drug paraphernalia.

- If all else fails, just keep doing what you're doing and time will tell the rest. Either he has truly stopped using or he will go deeper into the cycle of addiction and other signs and/or symptoms will emerge.

4.   We have a lot of alcoholism and drug addiction on both sides of our family. Are my children at higher risk for addiction?

The short answer is yes. Children of alcoholics or addicts are three times more likely to develop problems and, if both parents are addicts or alcoholics, the risk increases fivefold. This is due to heredity as well as learned behavior.

Because you have some great real-life examples at your fingertips, use them to talk to your kids about the dangers of drugs and how rampant addiction is in your family history. Explain to them they are at higher risk for addiction themselves because of this. Talk to them about the warning signs of alcoholism and/or drug addiction. Make sure they can always come to you for help or with questions.

Set zero tolerance expectations in your family for drug and alcohol use and stay informed about what is going on with teens in your community.

5.   Are alcoholism and drug addiction the same thing?

Yes – thcy arc the same disease process. Addiction is a chronic, progressive, relapsing disorder characterized by compulsive use of one or more substances that results in physical, psychological or social harm to the individual and continued use of the substance or substances despite this harm.

6.   What are some signs of alcoholism or addiction?

Some signs may be aggression, denial, depression or paranoia, emotional outbursts, poor motivation, inability to sit still, irritability, sweating, weight loss, excessive sleeping. See page 107 for a list of signs and symptoms of drug use. For more information, please go to www.theantidrug.com.

7.   I found pot in my teen's room – now what?

Act on it immediately. Stay calm and develop a game plan so that when you confront your teen you will be prepared for action.

- Obtain a drug test kit.

- Confront your teen at the earliest opportunity and be ready to administer the drug test.

- If the drug test is positive, call your health insurance company and research where you can take your teen for an assessment.

- Remind your teen you love him or her and will do whatever it takes to keep him or her safe.

- Levy consequences for your teen for having brought drugs into your home or for having a positive drug test.

- Be sure to destroy the marijuana and all drug paraphernalia.

- Disregard any claims by your son or daughter that the marijuana isn't his/hers.

8.   My teen tested positive on a drug test. How do I find a treatment facility in my area?

Start with your school counselor, school resource officer or family doctor. You can also visit www.findtreatment.samhsa.gov for help with this.

A drug treatment counselor is a professional who can properly assess whether your teen needs treatment. Remember, kids lie about drugs – don't buy it if your teen states the pot is not his or hers or says he's only smoked it once or twice. Better to be safe than sorry. If the counselor determines your teen does not have a serious problem warranting intervention, at least your teen got the message you are serious about drugs and alcohol and you have a zero tolerance for it in your home.

9.   My son refused to take a drug test. What do I do?

A child who has nothing to hide, hides nothing. A refusal equals a positive drug test. Follow the same recommendations as if he tested positive. Contact a drug treatment center and schedule an assessment.

10.   What do I do if my teenager refuses to meet with a drug treatment assessment counselor?

As the parent you have some control over the situation. Your number one priority must be to get your child to attend the assessment appointment. Withhold all privileges until your child agrees to go. This can include car, computer, cell phone, going out, etc—any privilege your teen values.

You may need an extra authority figure to help deliver your plan of action. This could include your school resource officer, school counselor or local law enforcement personnel.

Be patient, this may take some time. Don't give in. Once your teen realizes that you mean business and he is not going to get his privileges back, he will eventually agree to meet with a drug assessment counselor.

11.   I confronted my teenager about suspected drug use. Now he's run away. What do I do?

Usually kids run away as a threat to get you to back down from your rules. Calling the police and reporting him or her as a runaway sends the message to your teen that you are serious.

12.   I confronted my teen about her drug use and now she's missing. I don't want to call the police because I don't want my child to have a "record." How can I keep her out of the "system?"

A phone call to the police to report a runaway does not put your child into the "system." However, for some teens, getting into the system might be exactly what's needed to stop the cycle of drug use. I suggest you call the police and file a Missing Person Report. If you don't intervene now, your daughter may continue a downward spiral into drug addiction or worse. The juvenile justice system is designed for rehabilitation as opposed to the adult criminal justice system which focuses mainly on punishment. Early intervention is critical to successful intervention.

13.   My daughter told me the drugs I found in her car belonged to a friend. She said she'll be in danger if I confiscate the drugs. What do I do?

Do not believe her story. People who use drugs do not entrust them to others to "hold." People who don't do drugs rarely risk the consequences of drug possession for a friend. Act on it immediately. Stay calm and develop a game plan so that when you confront your teen, you will be prepared for action.

- Obtain a drug test kit.

- Confront your teen at the earliest opportunity and be ready to administer the drug test.

- If the drug test is positive, call your health insurance company and research where you can take your teen for an assessment.

- Remind your teen you love her and will do whatever it takes to keep her safe.

- Levy consequences for your teen for having brought drugs into your home or for having a positive drug test.

- Be sure to destroy the drugs and all drug paraphernalia.

- Disregard any claims by your daughter that the drugs weren't hers.

14. My son has suddenly started to hang around with some new friends that seem so different from his other friends. Should I be concerned?

Yes and no. A sudden change in friends can often be a warning sign of drug use. However, my first suggestion is to take the time to get to know the teens and trust your instincts before making a judgment. Do not allow your son to go to his new friends' homes without speaking to a parent first to determine their rules and supervision standards.

If, after getting to know his new friends, you still don't have a good feeling about them, pay attention to how your son's behavior changes with the new friends. If he becomes defiant or moody, has emotional outbursts or other behaviors not consistent with his usual personality, drug test your son.

15. I've caught my daughter drinking several times, but I never really thought it was much more than normal teen behavior – should I be concerned?

Yes. Remember, alcohol is a drug. It affects every part of the body, including the central nervous system and brain. Alcohol is the number one cause of death of teenagers. The younger a person starts drinking, the more at risk he/she is for developing alcohol dependence. Please take your daughter to a drug treatment counselor for a proper assessment to determine if your daughter needs further intervention.

16. My 10th grader, who used to get A's and B's on his report card, is now failing several courses. He just seems to lack motivation to do homework, or even turn in assignments. Could this be a symptom of drug use?

Failing grades are always a red flag for possible drug problems. If you haven't already drug tested your teen, that should be your first step. If you discover your teen is using drugs, follow through by having your teen assessed by a drug treatment counselor. Regardless of the drug test results, set up a meeting with your child's counselor at school to develop a plan of action the school can support.

In addition, I would recommend you look for a local chapter of Parent Project®, a parenting class that targets destructive adolescent behavior, including poor school performance. Check out www.parentproject.com for information.

17. I've had enough. I'm ready to give up. My son has been in and out of drug treatment and is out of control. I just want to send him somewhere to straighten him out. Where can I send him?

Don't give up. You are your child's best hope of recovery. First, you must find support for yourself. You can't do this alone. The road to recovery can be long, scary and disheartening. Nobody loves this child more than you do. You are his best hope for getting him on the road to recovery.

Second, check with the drug treatment counselor to see if a long-term treatment center is a good option for him. Explore this option carefully. Check out the Wilderness Treatment Center at www.wildernessaltschool.com in Montana. Or, check the Hazelden Center for Youth and Families in Minnesota at www.hazelden.org.

18. My son has been assessed and needs in-patient treatment. How much does it cost? How do I pay for it?

Drug treatment costs vary, depending on the needs of the patient and the type of treatment. Check with your employer to see if there is an Employee Assistance Program that may include coverage for the treatment. Medical insurance often covers treatment, so it's important to consult your family doctor and medical insurance carrier to determine your options.

If you don't have health insurance and your resources are limited, contact your county mental health department.

19. I've been struggling with my teen's addiction and I'm worn out. Where can I find family support programs locally?

Al-Anon (Alateen for younger members) offers hope and help to friends of alcoholics. Locate a local chapter at www.al-anon.alateen.org. You should be able to find a family education component through your teen's drug treatment center. Many churches also offer support.

20.   Teens are going to drink anyway. Wouldn't it be safer if I let them drink under my supervision and keep them off the highway?

Absolutely not! Remember, the earlier children begin drinking, the higher their risk of becoming alcohol dependent.

You are also assuming a high risk. All states in the United States have social host liability laws wherein adults can be prosecuted for serving alcohol to anyone under the age of 21. Liability can include medical bills and property damage. Parents who are not home can even be held accountable for underage drinking. Social host liability laws can apply to parents who don't take adequate steps to prevent teenage drinking in their homes.

21.   My 19-year-old son is living at home and he's using drugs. Is it too late to intervene?

No. It's never too late to try to save a loved one from drug dependency. If your son is dependent on you for support, you still have an opportunity and obligation to intervene regarding any destructive behavior.

When a child is over the age of 18, parents still have a lot of influence if they are supporting that child. Even though an 18-year-old is considered an adult and must agree to drug treatment, you can help steer him in the right direction by not giving him money or providing a soft place to "land." (your home, food, warm bed, etc.) If your child is using drugs, you must declare your home as a zero tolerance, drug-free zone. You must not let him live with you if he is unwilling to stop using drugs. You can tell him how much he is loved and how he has your full support after he has checked himself into treatment. This way you are offering your son help to get help, but not enabling him to continue a destructive life pattern.

RESOURCES

United States Department of Health and Human Services Substance Abuse and Mental Health Services Administration at www.samhsa.gov

SAMHSA finds substance abuse treatment facilities by location at www.findtreatment.samhas.gov/facilitylocatordoc.htm

National Institute on Drug Abuse at www.nida.nih.gov

NIDA for Teens at www.teens.drugabuse.gov

Parents. The Anti-Drug at www.theantidrug.com

Partnership for a Drug Free America at www.drugfreeamerica.org

Office of National Drug Control Policy at www.whitehousedrugpolicy.gov

Thousands of Alcoholism and Addiction Resources at www.SoberRecovery.com, www.druguse.com and www.drugfree.com

Residential Treatment Centers for Teens at www.selectown.com. Information about many options for parents of troubled teens, teens involved in drug abuse, and defiant teens including: treatment centers, boot camps, boarding schools, and military schools

Easy-to-understand information on drug testing your teen at www.drugtestyourteen.com

A parenting skills program designed specifically for parents with strong-willed or out-of-control children at www.Parentproject.com

INDEX

A

P

R